Nancy W. Collins is the assistant to the president of the Palo Alto Medical Foundation in California. Formerly, she was the assistant director of the Hoover Institution, and before that, the assistant director of the Sloan Executive Program of the Stanford Graduate School of Business. She holds a B.A. in Journalism and an M.S. in Personnel Administration, both from the University of North Carolina at Chapel Hill.

Prentice-Hall International, Inc., *London*
Prentice-Hall of Australia Pty. Limited, *Sydney*
Prentice-Hall Canada Inc., *Toronto*
Prentice-Hall of India Private Limited, *New Delhi*
Prentice-Hall of Japan, Inc., *Tokyo*
Prentice-Hall of Southeast Asia Pte. Ltd., *Singapore*
Whitehall Books Limited, *Wellington, New Zealand*
Editora Prentice-Hall do Brasil Ltda., *Rio de Janeiro*

NANCY W. COLLINS

Professional Women and Their Mentors

A Practical Guide to Mentoring
for the Woman
Who Wants to Get Ahead

A SPECTRUM BOOK

Prentice Hall, Inc., Englewood Cliffs, New Jersey 07632

Library of Congress Cataloging in Publication Data

Collins, Nancy W.
    Professional women & their mentors.

    "A Spectrum Book."
    Bibliography: p.
    Includes index.
    1. Women in the professions.   2. Mentors in the
professions.   3. Women in business.   4. Mentors in
business.   I. Title: II. Title: Professional women
and their mentors.
HD6054.C64   1983   658.4'09'088042   82-18573
ISBN 0-13-725994-8
ISBN 0-13-725986-7 (pbk.)

Excerpts from Daniel J. Levinson, The Seasons of a Man's Life,
*are reprinted by permission of the Sterling Lord Agency, Inc.
and Alfred A. Knopf, Inc. Copyright ©1978 by Daniel J. Levinson.*

1 2 3 4 5 6 7 8 9 10

ISBN 0-13-725994-8

ISBN 0-13-725986-7 (PBK.)

Cover design ©1983 by Jeannette Jacobs
Manufacturing buyer: Cathie Lenard

This Prentice-Hall book is available at a special discount when ordered
in bulk quantities. Contact: Prentice-Hall, Inc., General Publishing Division,
Special Sales, Englewood Cliffs, New Jersey 07632.

I am dedicating this book, with great affection, to my three former mentors: Frederick G. Atkinson, my first and most significant mentor, who early on was instrumental in my commitment to have a career; Carlton A. Pederson (now deceased), who let me know I could always count on his loyalty and support; and Mark D. Larkin, who encouraged and counseled me during a job change.

With gratitude, I would also like to dedicate this book to Lynne Lumsden, my acquisitions editor, who was helpful in my selection of Prentice-Hall as a publisher; Virginia H. McDowell, for her overall creative comments and insight in structuring the senior women's questionnaire on "Women as Mentors"; and Jacqueline E. Toth, for her many weekends of excellent editing and typing.

And finally, my personal support system was crucial in the writing of this book. Thus I am also dedicating it to the men in my life, my three sons: James Q. Collins, III, Charles L. Collins, and William R. Collins, with thanks for their understanding that while writing this book, my hectic schedule left little time for their mentoring...and to my friend and husband, Richard F. Chapman, M.D.

Contents

Preface

Professional Women and Their Mentors is written for the professional and managerial woman. It is a guide for women who are already working and have certain marketable skills, such as education, experience, and practical knowledge, and who have a strong desire to succeed.

For these competitive, assertive, and career-oriented women, this book will tell them how to get one step closer to the top. It will also have appeal for men who want to be better mentors to the women in their organization, and who need advice about the areas that will be the most beneficial.

This book has been written to inform and motivate professional women to take action in seeking the right mentor and in working more effectively with the one she has. It provides information on when an "apprenticeship" should end and how to detach oneself firmly from a mentor. It also advises on finding a new mentor on a higher level. This book is intended to be a resource of practical information on the entire "mentoring concept."

I decided to write this book after I attended a conference in San Francisco for professional women on the topic of "getting ahead." One of the subjects covered was mentors and the enormous impact that they can have on one's career, a topic which had interested me for years. The seminar leader stated that having a mentor could indeed make a crucial difference but that little had been written on this subject. When I surveyed the literature, I found that this was indeed true.

Thus I decided to design a questionnaire and conduct research of my own on a large group of professional women of achievement to study their mentoring relationships.

My sample consisted first of the membership of the Peninsula Professional Women's Network, a prestigious group of executive and professional women in the peninsula area from San Francisco to San Jose (with salaries basically ranging from $20,000 to over $100,000), and second, the membership of the Bay Area Executive Women's Forum (BAEWF), and elite San Francisco-based network. Last, I added professional women in several major cities throughout the United States.

Of the 600 questionnaires sent out, over 400 questionnaires were returned. As far as I know, this is the only sample of this size of professional women which studies their total mentoring relationships. From this group, twenty-four exceptional women were interviewed in depth during the summer of 1981. Although many moved to even higher positions soon after (and some to new organizations), I have kept their titles and all facts consistent to reflect their status when I met with them. They were selected as examples of women who well illustrated specific phases of the mentoring process and were willing to share their experiences. All of the case names and organizations (except one where I used a pseudonym) are real; the mentors' names have all been changed in spite of the fact that some wished to be identified. Out of this research, certain interesting and valid conclusions have been drawn.

Through the questionnaire, I discovered that almost all of the women had exclusively male mentors, so I use the male gender when referring to mentors. However, as women continue to progress, not only are they beginning to have female mentors, but female mentors are mentoring to men as well. The protégée, or younger person receiving the mentoring, is referred to as a "mentoree." This is a word which I created while writing this book.

In compiling the information from the survey, I could not help but notice that *all* of the women in the study reaffirmed their beliefs in the positive aspects of the mentor relationship. What I learned was what professional men have known for a long time—that having an experienced person guide your career gives you both the assistance and the connections necessary to get ahead. I also learned another well-kept male secret—that the mentor relationship goes far beyond the work situation and the transmittal of new skills. I discovered that it can literally change one's life and reach into areas totally unconnected with the workplace. Through their mentor relationship, the respondees were lifted to heights never before dreamed of or ever thought possible.

I wrote this book in my three favorite cities—San Francisco, New York, and New Orleans. I have experienced the joy of living, working, being at my creative best, and making significant and life-long friends in each of these places. Thus it seems only proper that different parts of this book be conceived in all three cities.

"Come to the edge," he said.
They said, "We are afraid."
"Come to the edge," he said.
They came.
He pushed them...and they flew

Guillaume Apollinaire

Introduction

WOMEN IN THE WORK FORCE

There are over 43 million women in the work force today; they have a median age of 34 and constitute more than two-fifths of the workers. A total of 62 percent of all women work, compared with 88 percent of all men. Women in general are concentrated in low-paying, dead-end jobs, and as a result, earn about three-fifths of what men do. Women with four years of college earn less than men with an eighth-grade education. Although earnings parity with men is closer in professional fields, even those women are still at the lower end of their pay scales. In fact, the U.S. Department of Labor estimated that in 1980 women in managerial jobs had a median salary of only 55 percent of that earned by men. Women hold only 6 percent of top-level administrative positions, and we don't need a calculator to tell us, then, that 94 percent of these top jobs are held by men. Also, an even smaller number of women are in other large organizational positions of real power, such as corporate board memberships, presidents, key vice presidents, controllers of the purse strings, or even managers of large numbers of people or other resources. Why? Women simply have not been given the proper help, training, or coaching to compete successfully in the professional world.

If women want to succeed, they need to be mentored into these positions traditionally held by men. With a suitable tutor, women will have a much greater chance of understanding the game called "working." Men understand and play it well. Using a mentor must not be confused with intelligence, hard work, or ability, but if one has these attributes, a mentor can make the critical difference in her rise to the top. As Louis Pasteur said, "Chance favors only the prepared mind."

The shortage of female role models adds to the limited feedback that younger women need to climb upward. Nor have there been the large numbers of women on a peer level to form "teams" and utilize the "buddy system." In such a "system," the sharing of information, needing one another, cultivating colleagues (both peers and superiors), and helping each other automatically are the basic functions of the "Old Boys' Network." This feeling of belonging to a supportive group sustains men during their entire working career.

Once a woman makes a commitment to have a professional life, she needs to seek an advocate who is senior. This person will counsel and support her, assist her in her climb upward, introduce her, and give her vision. For the mentoring relationship to continue, she needs to show that she can capitalize on such attention; she also needs, in an intangible way, to further the career of her mentor, for a mentor's gratification is not solely in watching her succeed.

MY THREE MENTORS

I have learned that for an ambitious woman, such as myself, a mentor is even more crucial to her career than to her male counterpart's. Looking back on my own working life, I realize that I have had a new mentor about every eight to ten years. All have been men, and all were ten to fifteen years older. The relationship with each one was different, and necessary for that stage of my personal growth and development.

I was in my early twenties when I moved to New York City and met my first mentor. I had just graduated from the University of North Carolina and was working for a large Fortune 500 corporation where he was a senior vice president. I did not work directly for him, and I worked for that company only a short time, but his contribution to my career has lasted my entire life. By his own purpose and professional example, he helped to shape my personal philosophy and to formulate my desire to have a serious career, not merely a job. Not only was he greatly revered by everyone in the organization, but he took the time to show a personal interest in younger people's growth and development. So often, one's first mentor is the most important; he can, and sometimes without knowing it, change your life. Certainly this was true for me.

In addition, he gave me vision, taught me to "think big," and to see the whole picture. I am still amazed when I see so many professional people, especially mid-level and higher, who "think small." Through my mentor, I got a glimpse of what it was like to be influential, on national committees, and to serve the government. I sensed his excitement of working with dynamic and intelligent people who were in policy-making roles.

This mentor still follows my career, and we write and occasionally see each other. He expressed interest in this book, and in several places I have quoted relevant comments of his regarding mentorship. Although he stopped acting as my mentor long ago, I find myself still thinking about him and how he might counsel me in certain situations.

My second mentor relationship occurred when I was in my early thirties. This mentor was director of a program, in which I became the assistant director, at the Stanford University Graduate School of Business. He selected me and gave me an opportunity to put into action certain skills and strategies that I had been accumulating. He assigned me total responsibility for some segments of the program, saying that in these areas "the buck stops with you." When I had a conflict or problem, although it remained unsaid, he let me know that he was always there and I could count on his loyalty and support. On one memorable occasion, he challenged the dean on my behalf and won. This solid backing was a new experience for me and one that I will never forget. He also taught me to ask for the final responsibility and authority that comes with managing a project, which was not always given to women. He wrote textbooks of national prominence and was on several boards, but his main satisfaction was in interacting with his wife, two sons, and many grandchildren, and he let it be known that he valued that part of his life above all else.

What were his other contributions to my career? He gave me a lot of encouragement, shared my aspirations, and appeared to have absolute faith in my ability. I would not have disappointed or let him down for anything in the world. He also guided me at the beginning of my first "power struggle" and offered advice on office politics and the male ego. When he died several years ago, it was an emotionally devastating experience. Although at the time of his death he was no longer acting as my mentor, I knew that no one else could ever again take his particular place in my career.

My third and final mentor relationship occurred when I was in my early forties. This influential man lived and worked in San Francisco. He is a CPA and a recognized authority in the field of corporate taxation. He recently moved to New York and is now responsible for his firm's worldwide expatriate tax practice. While we never worked together, his main contribution was to help me get my career in focus. He gave me excellent advice on making a job change, and the shove that made me do it. This mentor reinforced the fact of how important it is to take advantage of the unexpected opportunities as they come along. We also discussed possibilities for my serving on several committees in the Bay Area and the positive visibility that would follow. He was one of the few people at that time I could count on to be totally honest and open with me. Here was someone I could do "reality testing" with: Were my ideas good ones? How were others perceiving me? Sometimes this candor can be painful as well as positive, but it is necessary if one is to progress beyond a certain level.

He also taught me how important it is to take professional risks, and at one point, he helped me deal with a crisis. He also taught me to expect professional calamities from time to time. Men, from early boyhood, seem to be put in positions in which they experience disappointments; perhaps this occurs through the milieu of male competition and team sports—half win while half lose. Men seem to know that there will be other chances, that losses are temporary, and consequently they seem to bounce back more quickly. They also seem to know that not everyone is going to like them, and, faced with ambivalent work relationships, men seem to handle themselves more successfully.

Through discussions with my mentor, he reinforced the importance of learning from a loss and preparing for the next time. He was pleased to be mentioned in this book, and sent the following quote: "Good judgment comes from experience, good experience comes from bad judgment." As a woman, it is important during a traumatic work time to have someone believe in you, to reinforce your belief in yourself, and to say that not only does he know you will survive but that you will land on your feet in an even higher place. And this was what my third mentor was able to do for me.

CHAPTER ONE

What Is a Mentor?

Virginia's mentor was very, very demanding. He would hand her books and papers to read and expect her to discuss them as a peer. When she was looking at a declining job market for Ph.D's, she knew she would not have had as many interviews without his strong letters of recommendation. Later, he also supported her move from academia to banking.

Judith's mentor spent time with her each day. When the market started in the morning, he'd proudly say, "There she goes!" Later, he changed firms and called her to go back to work for him, giving her the opportunity to become a registered broker.

During the time Alice worked for her mentor, he developed her skills as a manager. The projects she worked with him on were the first things she had done since getting out of school. Two of the things he did were to make her the head of the department and to give her a raise as well as a new title. He also taught her the fundamentals of how to work with people and guide the development of their potential. Later, she realized how especially lucky she was to have had his guidance at the beginning.

It appears that everyone who writes about mentors has his or her own definition. Webster, a good place to start, defines a mentor as a "trusted counselor or guide, a tutor or coach." In Greek mythology, the wise old Mentor was asked by Ulysses to advise and watch after his son, Telemachus, when Ulysses left on his famous ten-year odyssey. In fact, Mentor simply became a surrogate father, offering the young, vulnerable boy guidance, support, and love until his father returned.

In a professional sense, powerful mentor figures can make a critical difference in one's career. They are important not only at the beginning and the mid-levels but to provide a final push into senior positions. As corporate attitudes change, women are beginning to be allowed to penetrate all levels of decision making. The whole system of sponsorship has traditionally been reserved for men, and it has only recently included women in any significant numbers. Margaret Hennig and Anne Jardin, in *The Managerial Woman,* found that male supporters, first fathers and then mentors, played key roles in encouraging women to achieve in fields long dominated by men. They told women who wanted to get ahead to "look for a coach, a godfather or godmother, a mentor, or an advocate."[1]

When referring to mentors in this book, I will use the male gender. Due to the distribution of power and influence in the professional world, most mentors, of both men and women, have been men. Certainly this was true in my research. It is interesting to note further that the more outstanding a woman is in her field, the more outstanding her mentor seems to have been.

After my research, I have concluded that the following five criteria are necessary if one is to be defined as a mentor, or one who can provide upward mobility to a professional career. Although ideally all five criteria are present, because the mentor relationship is not a permanent one, different combinations are possible (even preferable) as one's career evolves. Also, a woman's first mentor may well be her most important one. This person is the first to introduce her to her new professional life, and can by his interaction provide the basis for the way she molds her own career.

[1]Margaret Hennig and Anne Jardin, *The Managerial Woman* (New York: Anchor Press/Doubleday, 1977).

HIGHER UP ON THE ORGANIZATIONAL LADDER   What are the criteria, then, for mentorship? First, a mentor must be higher up on the professional ladder than the woman he is to mentor. No matter how much you like or admire someone, he cannot be below you on the organizational chart if he is to be a true mentor. Women need different strategies for success than men. They do not always get sufficient knowledge in their college training of the complex way the professional world operates. Mentors need to be higher ranking in order to assist you in your climb.

AN AUTHORITY IN HIS/HER FIELD   Second, a mentor must also be a recognized authority in his field; he must be clearly established in the area in which he is to mentor. And almost always, the mentor is older than the mentoree; certainly he must be ahead in experience and knowledge. Often much of the work day can be unexpected. The results achieved are, to some extent, bound to how you can handle the impromptu. The mentor, with his experience and knowledge, can help you deal with the planned work load as well as with the unplanned, and can answer questions and give information in areas which are unfamiliar.

INFLUENTIAL   Next, a mentor must be influential. If he is to make an impact on your career, he must have a recognized "voice" in the profession and be close to the lines of authority and power. Mentors usually have a long track record of being influential leaders, which can usually be traced back as far as their academic and collegiate activities. If he goes to bat for you, he needs to be in a position to carry it off.

INTERESTED IN YOUR GROWTH AND DEVELOPMENT   Fourth, a mentor needs to have a genuine interest in your personal growth and development. He should like and respect you as a person, be able to see your potential, and feel that your development will not only be good for you but for the organization. While some mentors are transitional figures, they give tangible assistance to various stages of your advancement. Other mentors remain interested in you and your career for a lifetime.

WILLING TO COMMIT TIME AND EMOTION TO THE RELATIONSHIP   And last, but not least, a mentor should be willing to commit time and emotion to the relationship. This goes beyond mere interest and is a commitment that, more often than not, is intense. A mentoring relationship can be one of great devotion. There is mutual trust and caring, confidentiality, and a willingness to develop and foster the relationship. It takes time to discuss both fears and problems, as well as to share victories and successes.

When I asked one of my mentors what he thought a mentor relationship was, this was his reply:

> "The mentor relationship does not readily lend itself to vivisection or definition of its components. It's somewhat like trying to define what constitutes a friend or what a friend 'does.' The relationship is formal and impersonal, yet constructive and of great use. Perhaps the most valuable thing a mentor does is to help the young person grasp the difference between what's really important and what only seems so—in other words, perspective."

A mentor is all these things—and more.

WHAT A MENTOR IS NOT

The mentor just discussed also felt it important to make clear what a mentor is not.

AUTOMATICALLY A PAL   After much thought, he states, "It would be a mistake to assume that your mentor is automatically a pal or a close friend." Thus you cannot expect social invitations or to mix with his family and friends. If the relationship grows, you *can* be included in his personal life, but you should not take this for granted, and it may never happen.

"ON CALL" FOR GRIEVANCES AND FRUSTRATIONS   "He is not 'on call' to listen to your imagined grievances or real frustrations. If he has experience, judgment, and an interest in helping young people develop their best talents, you are probably not his first or his last mentoree." You can count on your mentor to discuss the major problems and tactics, but don't impose on him to listen and counsel you on all minor ones.

EXCLUSIVELY YOURS   "Nor is he exclusively yours; he may well be observing and helping other younger employees who appear to have a high potential for growth and advancement. If he is a competent executive, he will have learned to conserve his own time. He may well be affording encouragement, admonitions, opportunities, and challenging assignments to other promising young persons at the same time.

"Your mentor may perceive your charm but he is more interested in your initiative, your competence, your accomplishments, and your ability to work effectively with others—your peers, your superiors, and your subordinates.

"If you are alert and responsive, you may, in a sense, 'select' your mentor. He is not, however, someone you cleverly recruit to give you special advantages. More likely, the reverse will be the case. He will have taken note of you because of your superior performance in the work assigned to you. He takes an interest, not because you are assertive and aggressive or transparently on the hunt for a mentor; but because you have distinguished yourself as intelligent, competent, diligent, good-humored, and tactful."

NOT TO BE GRACEFULLY DISMISSED   "Finally, your mentor is not someone you just gracefully dismiss when you decide the relationship is no longer useful to you. (This may be necessary if his interest in you patently exceeds the bounds of propriety, but this would be a rare exception.) The mentor relationship has a natural life cycle of its own, not a predictable span of time but a function of individual growth and changing circumstances. You should be able to sense when it is phasing out and avoid the error of 'trying to make yesterday last a little longer.'"

MENTORS VERSUS ROLE MODELS AND HELPFUL PEERS

Mentors should not be confused with helpful peers or role models. Helpful peers are more or less on the same level. Although they can be very encouraging and give supportive insight, by definition they are not superior and are not in a position to influence your career with the impact that a true mentor can. Their help is through the sharing of their experiences. They may warn you of pitfalls and offer guidance around obstacles. They can discuss personalities and share their knowledge of the profession. They can tell you *their* perception of your situation, demeanor, and even discuss voice and professional dress codes.

Role models do not function as mentors, but mentors can function as role models. Role models are impressive and important figures in the distance. You can admire, emulate, respect, and almost worship the person, but the role model doesn't necessarily have to know that you exist. Or if they do, role models do not make a commitment to your career. There is not the give-and-take, close contact, or interface found in a mentor relationship. Any aid they provide to a career is by example only, not by giving direct advice, recommending one for promotion, spending time together discussing work, or caring about you as an individual. Even if you have mentors, it is important to have role models—they also help you to grow. It is important to watch people who are effective at what they do well. Successful people are always figuring out creative and innovative ways to do things, and you can learn a great deal observing successful role models.

CASES

The three cases of Virginia, Judith, and Alice that follow were selected to illustrate what is meant by a mentor.

> *Virginia H. McDowell, Ph.D.*
> Planning Analyst
> Corporate Planning
> Bank of the West

"I met my mentor, Dr. J. David Duncan, in January of 1971 when I transferred to the University of California, Santa Cruz, and enrolled in a small seminar he was teaching on "The Psychological Aspects of Self-Determination." He had a lasting influence on me. Deep and profound changes in my thinking and my life would come about as a result of my relationship with him over the next six years. He was fifty-two at the time and had just been appointed vice chancellor. I was unaware of his position (I had yet to sort out the people and titles) and had picked the course because the topic appealed to me. After fourteen years as a full-time wife and mother, I had returned to school and had concluded that there had been very little self-determination in my life to that point.

"The seminar dragged, and after a few weeks I went to David's office to talk about it. He agreed with most of what I said (such as more participation and discussion), and as a result, the seminar changed direction after that. That was the beginning of the relationship, and I felt quite comfortable with him then. Later in the course we began to read some of his work, and I discovered that he was one of the top social psychologists in the United States. I was somewhat awed by that and uneasy with him. Had I known who he was from the start I doubt the relationship would have evolved the way it did. My awe lessened over the next year and a half as I worked with him in independent study and wrote a senior honors thesis. Over time, mutual respect replaced my uneasiness.

"David was very, very demanding. He would hand me books and papers to read and expect me to discuss them as a peer. This meant hours of additional reading to fill myself in on the background of whatever he handed me. He would ask me what I thought about a particular writer on theory, and I would immerse myself in it to be able to discuss it with him. Of course, in this process I began to question everything, and when we met every few weeks he would validate that and push the questioning process further.

"I think David recognized and confirmed my abilities before they were believably real to me. He told me not only could I write, but that I wrote very well and he was very explicit about how I could hone that skill. He critiqued my work, wrote all over it, commenting, correcting things, asking questions. He taught me how to address myself to the strengths and weaknesses of a paper in a systematic and thorough way. Later, my students had similar things to say about my critiques of their work. He gave me a large commitment of time in a very busy travel, teaching, and administrative schedule, and I was conscious of how I spent that time and arrived at each session with copious notes and an internal agenda of questions.

"Shortly after I entered UCSC, a female instructor of mine asked me where I was going to graduate school. At that time it had not occurred to me to go to graduate school—I was very focused on the present. I mentioned this to David and he said, 'I assumed, of course, that you were going.' Later I asked him why *he* hadn't suggested it, and I said I thought he would have had I been a male student. He agreed with that, reluctantly, and that was one of the first confrontations around the issue of his chauvinism. After that he was full of suggestions about graduate school—of whom to call, what to say—and he wrote a powerful letter of recommendation for me.

"I recall one incident from that time very vividly; I was interested in applying to a particular Ph.D. program on campus and had gone in to see the professor who chaired it. I do not remember exactly how he asked the question about my family, but I told him I was married, was 37, and had four children. He asked their ages (five to thirteen) and then there was a long pause. Finally, he remarked: 'The University is for scholars; you are too old to become one; furthermore, you belong at home with your children.' I was stunned and left the room, choking back tears. I met David in an adjacent corridor. He asked me what had happened and I told him. He said, 'What nonsense. He always was a silly old fool. Don't pay any attention as he won't be there next quarter when you apply.'

"In graduate school I had a dual matriculation on two University of California campuses, so I continued to work with David. It was at this point that he began to give me rough drafts of his work to read and critique. This was very valuable as I could then see the writing process from beginning to end. During this period he became president of the APA (American Psychological Association) and his sphere of influence increased. I was very conscious of that—worried about "using" him and would check this out from time to time. Looking back, I think that was rather silly—few male students would have worried about that! He would never dig things out for me (teaching fellowships, grants, etc.) but would support strongly anything I found for myself and wanted to do. When I finished my thesis and it looked like a publishable book, he wrote a strong review of it and sent that off with the manuscript and it was published. During my final year of graduate school I was applying for teaching positions, and he wrote a very strong cover letter for me. I know I would not have had the interviews I did (particularly in the declining job market that existed) without his letter. His opinion of my worth carried a great deal of weight.

"The most valuable part of the graduate school experience was the constant feeling that he was treating me like an intellectual peer and it was believable! I also knew at a very deep level that he respected me and valued me as a person and was keenly interested in my growth. Throughout the six-year period he maintained a gentle, but firm and very constant pressure that continually challenged me to learn and understand and to see things from multiple perspectives. He seemed to me to be devoid of bias (except for some traditional sex-role biases of which he was largely aware) and therefore, my own biases stood out to me in stark contrast and I was forced to confront them continually. He had a profound influence on my life and career. In honesty, he is certainly partly responsible for my career; he helped me develop my intellectual skills and those skills I use daily and value tremendously—I remember what life was like without them! I have a freedom to think and choose and I think that was partly a result of my relationship with him over that period. Others influenced my thinking and made valuable contributions, but his was the most significant.

"Just as I came to appreciate the power of his intellect, I also came to value him as a person. I admired his balance (and still do), a certain unflappability that enables him to sort out people and situations, and his basic honesty about himself and his world. In short, I became fond of him and I knew he was fond of me and that presented problems during my final year of graduate school. My work was not a problem—in some respects he became tougher about it as I neared the end—but my emotions were. I was definitely pulled, as he was, and it was hard to deal with that. After I left graduate school, we worked that out and decided to remain friends (rather than lovers) and have remained significant persons in each others' lives.

"Four years later when I made the decision to leave academia, he supported that. I spent several months looking at alternatives before joining Bank of the West. I now have a newly created and very challenging position in corporate planning, and I work very closely with a man who took an early retirement from a large eastern bank and is an internal consultant with my bank. He has a wealth of technical knowledge and has taken an interest in my progress in banking. He gives me things to read and frequent mini-lectures on various aspects of banking. As I have no background in finance, this has been invaluable. He has also suggested activities for me to carry out that place me in fairly constant contact with the senior management of the bank and has encouraged me to take risks and to ask questions.

"I am very much aware of the opportunity that I have—much more so than I was ten years ago—and I am able to ask directly for the kinds of information and *coaching* that will enable me to grow fast in my work. I really feel like I have a cheering section at the bank, rooting for me to succeed. That is really a nice feeling!

"I have had some women mentors in graduate school and earlier, but they were not in a position to do for me what the men were able to do. They did not have the influence; they did what they could and *encouraged* me (they contributed to my survival), but they were not as deeply challenging as the men. I think that this is why I try to be challenging to the women who are referred to me—particularly Ph.D.s and Ed.Ds from academia who are trying to move into the business world.

"Of course, I am supportive, too, but I try to push them a little, try to get them to stretch a bit and believe that they can do it. Most of the women that I see are about ten to fifteen years younger than I am, and I get them to look at their track records and see what they have done. I believe that they can have the best of both worlds, although it is damned difficult. I have just begun to have the opportunity to refer women along the network I have established, and I feel really pleased when I can do that—encourage and challenge them as well as open some doors."

Judith Briles
Judith Briles & Company
Financial Planning

"Robert Packman was my most significant mentor. I met him in 1969 when I was working in Los Angeles as a secretary for a brokerage firm, Bateman Eichler, Hill Richards, in order to supplement the family income. I had married early, at 16, and had children soon after, so at that time I had little formal education; later I earned my M.B.A. from Pepperdine.

"Several different kinds of things were happening during this time. I did not have a good marriage, and I had joined and become very involved in an international sorority, Beta Sigma Phi. I discovered that I was the lead person in sales for ads in Southern California for the sorority, but did not realize the significance others attributed to that at the time. It was only later that I knew I was finally in a career that fitted my earlier skills and sense of personal enjoyment and fulfillment. I was brought up in a family that did not talk about finance or business; however, the family I married into was very successful, very entrepreneurial, and discussed stocks and other financial matters. I liked that, and I liked what money could do—I wanted to have money.

"When I worked at Bateman, Rob, my mentor, spent time each working day with me. I was very loyal to him and liked him very much. In school, I had excelled in math, and I had liked numbers since early childhood. So, when the market started in the morning, it was like, 'There she goes!'—like a horse race. Client contact was fun. I like helping them out, wanted to know more about the companies and why we recommended those particular ones. In early 1970, the market continued to decline, and we were not as busy or as profitable. It was during this period that Rob was able to spend a lot of time going over various factions of the market and what makes it tick. We discussed stock market areas such as convertible bonds, warrants, over-the-counter market options, and balance sheets. I started taking home brochures to study and learn more.

"I also found that when I put my own systems in, I was much more valuable as a secretary, so I worked at having indispensable files and notes. However, in spite of this, when I asked for a raise of fifty dollars, the manager said 'no.' Then the whole floor went to bat for me, and I got it.

"At the time, I didn't think of becoming a broker, because that wasn't something women did then, and it never dawned on me to do such a thing or that it was even an option. I thought of myself as a mother first, but I took home all the New York Stock Exchange brochures and continued to read. In mid-1970, many people were laid off, including me, so I went home and compensated by having another baby (who later died).

"While I was recovering from this deep personal loss, Rob changed firms and went to a larger one with more visibility and with very successful people—people who had made it big. During this time, we had stayed in contact, and one day he called and asked me to go back to work for him. He offered more pay and less hours! So I accepted, and got a raise to $625 per month in 1971. This seemed like a lot!

"The new firm wanted the women to be registered; this was better than the old firm, and also we sometimes got a percentage of the broker's business. I have always had goals and objectives that were measurable, and I gave myself two months to take the test to become registered—thank heavens I passed. I would study for the test from 10 p.m. to 2 a.m., the only time I had available. At this time I had three children and my marriage was really falling apart—then my husband threw me a bomb by deciding he was not going to work anymore.

"Bateman Eichler, Hill Richards got in touch with me, and I took a practice test with them and passed. They offered me a job in their Torrance office, which was "in my back yard," versus driving into Los Angeles every day. I was to do the research, cold calling, and also act as the manager's secretary. During this time, my marriage bottomed out, and finally I asked for a divorce. As a result of my personal life, I got fired! Today, a company would not have gotten away with this discriminatory nonsense. I had never been fired before, and it bruised my ego. I looked for other jobs, and I found out I was overqualified for the openings I approached, yet I still assumed I could only do clerical support functions.

"When I interviewed with E. F. Hutton in Torrance for a secretarial position, I was told I was overqualified, but that they would be interested in me as a broker. My male friends who were brokers were excited and said, 'Of course you should do this. We are angry you are not already in this position.' At this time I was registered and had been doing cold calling and research. The dissolution of my marriage was awful, and during this time a judge ordered my husband and me to continue living in the same house with joint custody of the children. One day my husband threw me down the stairs, and I finally left. Establishing credit was difficult as my husband canceled all my credit cards, even though they had been obtained on my credit history. I finally decided to leave the area for good. Friends put me on an airplane, and I flew to San Francisco. I had fifty dollars, and the only hotel I had heard of in San Francisco was the Fairmont. You can imagine how far my money went there!

"I began my interviews, and E. F. Hutton said they would hire me, as did every firm I interviewed with. Their risk was minimal because, after all, I was already registered. I came out of of my divorce with my sanity, my three children, but no money. I finally decided to settle on the San Francisco Peninsula because of my children, the weather, and the composite of the residents already here. This area had a lot of growth and new wealth, and I felt it would be easier to be the 'new kid on the block.'

"The biggest single thing I learned during this time was to tell my clients when things are bad, and to be open and honest with them. Many people got financially wiped out during this time, and it was difficult. When I joined Hutton, I was their 'token' woman on the Peninsula. Soon I made over $10,000 a month in commission, and male brokers were still implying "they knew how I got it," which was and is nonsense—I know few women who will compromise just to be successful. I learned later, through experience, that this kind of reply is one of jealousy.

"In 1976 I was seriously ill and had time to do a lot of thinking. In the mid-seventies, I was telling people to get out of the market and put their money elsewhere. In 1977, I sat down with one of the vice presidents of EFH who was regional sales manager and said, 'What are my options with this firm?' I did not know where I was going, but I knew I was going somewhere big. He said, 'There are really no options, but you can be a branch office coordinator for a product, such as annuities or insurance.' This answer gave me the freedom to leave with zero guilt, and this in itself can be a turning point in one's career. So I wrote down all my options, looking into the risks and the rewards. At this point, I had been with Hutton for five years and two weeks. When I originally joined the firm, I had made an internal commitment of five years to learn and make mistakes. After being with EFH for one year, I knew I wanted to return to the smaller regional or boutique type of firm.

"When I evaluated the risks and rewards, word got out that I was looking, and several companies, including my previous affiliates, approached me to join them or to open up a new branch office. EFH was not aware that I was investigating other opportunities. The brokerage business is the only one I know in which notice is not given by the sales staff. You resign when you are prepared to walk out the door, otherwise they take your books, change the locks, and make life miserable for you. EFH was hurt but was halfway pleasant when they found out I was leaving. I called or wrote principal men in the firm and thanked them for the opportunity of working with them. Little did they know that I would take clients with me or that my new enterprise would be competitive with EFH. They were not as pleasant when accounts began to transfer to Judith Briles & Company.

"In January 1978, I opened up my own company. We have grown to a staff of fifteen. People have shown great moral support during this time, such as my former mother-in-law (who is wonderful), professional colleagues, and friends.

"During my earlier career, Rob was my main mentor. Looking back, I can say that he took the time to make me aware of my working environment, and he gave me the freedom to ask questions without feeling stupid. I was hungry enough then to want to know. I have kept up with him, but the mentor relationship has ended. Probably now there is a reverse as I am on my own and way ahead of a lot of people who were ahead of me before.

"I never thought of looking to a woman to act as my mentor because they just weren't there in my field. When I decided to open my own business, some of the men said the risks were too great, but my women friends said, 'Go for it!' My former mentor, Rob, said, 'Why not?' and 'You have little to lose as you go along.' One of my good as well as negative sides is that I am fair and very trusting. I have discovered that this can get you into trouble! Another important element was that I didn't know I could *not* succeed.

"Those who have made it up to higher levels find it hard to get other mentors. Most of us are colleagues, peers. We aren't really nurtured because we have already made it, and there are fewer women at the very top to act as support system or teaching vehicle. One of my concerns as a mentor for other women is that I sometimes feel drained. I can't spread myself around, and I know that these women need the support to encourage them to take risks, to go for it.

"Most successful women feel that mentors are important at some segment in their lives. Although many women are entering the investment fields, their failures unfortunately appear to be more visible than those of their male counterparts. Maybe women can get there on their own 'stumbling,' but they would have to be very strong to get through the pitfalls when they come. In my business, with so many appalling failures, especially early on, guidance can be essential."

Alice MacNaughton
Special Events Director
Emporium-Capwell Company

"My mentor, Paul Burgess, came into the Emporium Capwell Company at approximately the same time that I did. He headed up a division where I was the assistant to the department head. After my mentor had been with the company for about six months, he began to make a lot of changes. One of the things he did was to make me head of the department, and to give me a raise as well as a new title. I had a lot of respect for him and worked hard to help build the Special Events area. I started working for Paul about six years ago, and worked for him for about four years. He is now senior vice president, Sales Promotion, for another department store.

"The age difference between us is about fourteen years. During the time I worked for Paul, he developed my skills as a manager. He taught me the fundamentals of how to work and develop people. The projects that I worked on with him were the first things that I had done after getting out of school, so all of my experience was new, and I felt that I was especially lucky to have his guidance at the beginning.

"I really liked Paul. We sparked ideas off each other. One of the reasons that he became my mentor was that we produced a lot of exciting promotions together. My ideas played off his ideas. I'd like to think that we were known as a team. He was the leader, but when people thought of Special Events, they thought of both of us. The job association lasted about four years, and then he left his position and became director of stores, which moved him to another department within the company. By that time, my abilities as a manager had grown significantly, and there comes a time in all mentor relationships when it is time to move on. Your mentor has other people that he needs to help, and you need to grow in other directions and on your own.

"Paul's change in jobs, then, came just at the right time for me. It was a mutual parting of the ways. During this period, my own ideas were developing, and I had the opportunity to work with a new boss who had different ideas and perspectives.

"Paul and I still keep in touch occasionally, but I don't call him for advice because we work in competitive businesses. One factor, typical of mentor relationships, was that what Paul taught me is all that he is ever going to teach me, and if I wanted to get ahead and develop, I needed to realize this. I have to take the initiative, and I don't need to ask for his advice anymore.

"For Paul's career, perhaps I was a spark. I certainly had a lot of enthusiasm in those days, and people genuinely seemed to like to work with me. We staged some successful events and our endeavors fostered new ideas and contacts. Those whom we met from outside our company were among our greatest supporters.

"Paul taught me a lot about being a mentor, and I am being a mentor now to other women. There is an unofficial businesswomen's network (in San Francisco), and women whom I've met now call me on a regular basis to let me know where they are and what they are doing. I try to give them suggestions about their career, others they should meet, and new ideas to think about. Today, women seem to be more open. You realize after a while that women are all in this together. Making someone else unsuccessful doesn't mean you will make it youself.

"I have another mentor now with whom I am beginning to develop a strong relationship—a high-level woman who lives in the area. She has been interested in getting me involved in other activities, and she would like to see me leave the retail field and go into another business, such as banking. I would like to move from special events into marketing or another phase. She has been very helpful in introducing me to people, and in just calling me up to see how I am doing and what my ideas are. I not only value her advice, but her personal friendship as well.

"My new mentor is a very successful businesswoman who likes to keep in touch with younger people, learn what their ambitions are, where they are going, and what they are doing. She feels that she is successful by helping other women succeed. She believes in my management ability, and I have also worked with her husband on a professional basis.

"A situation unique to my mentor situation relates to Paul. He really taught me to be patient, but I don't think impatience in young people is that unusual. I was always impatient to get somewhere quicker, do it faster, and this knowledge of me was important in our relationship. Paul protected me a great deal in the beginning when I was extremely naive about how people operated politically. I might have said something that was not appropriate, and Paul protected me from any repercussions.

One of the interesting aspects of the ending of our relationship was that I didn't want to be "protected" anymore. I felt strong enough to take it head on and deal with it.

"My boss after Paul stood by me, but let me take any repercussions. I think Paul's support gave me the impetus to keep on trying. In the earlier times it was easier to give up, and he taught me to follow through and persevere. Paul was good at pushing me and getting me a good salary increase every year.

"We have a committee in our company called the operating committee, made up of the top sixty members of management. By the time I was named to this committee, people were surprised to see the notice. Many of them said, 'We always thought you were already on the operating committee.' Paul helped me to create the perception so that when things happened for me, people thought they were happening all along. I now think that I was too young at a certain point and would have been open to criticism had these successes come sooner.

"During the years that I worked for Paul, our department grew from two to seven people, and our budget responsibilities doubled. Also, my rank and power in the company grew tremendously. I have a woman for a boss today, which is the first time I have ever worked for a female. I think she will allow me a great deal of flexibility, independence, and a lot of growth. The people in upper management know that I am looking for upward mobility. I believe my new boss will be a most supportive person in my career.

"For months and months I had a dream that there was a train going through my life and I was always missing the train. I would keep running and running and could never catch it. Finally, Paul made me realize that the train was me, and that I was never going to miss the train, but that I was trying so hard for a long period to 'do good and keep up.' When I got appointed to the operating committee and got a big raise, all of a sudden I was at rest. I felt that I had arrived, and I stopped having those dreams. Once I got there, I didn't miss the train. But now that I feel it is time for me to move on to other things, I may start having that dream again. I know my need to feel that I am doing my best, and it frightens me."

CHAPTER TWO

What a Mentor Does

The most significant thing Nancy's mentor did for her was to take a risk himself in giving her a promotion over others who looked more qualified on paper. Later, she realized he had set her career up beautifully, and she knew absolutely that she could not have gotten to this high level without him.

Diane's mentor tried to assess where she was and what she needed, and then provide advice and counsel. He was delighted with her initiative and the results of projects she did on her own. Later, she left his company and the relationship ended. But she finds it very valuable to trade ideas and talk with him often about her work.

Virginia's mentor employed her at the low point in her life. He boosted her self-esteem by complimenting her work and having belief in her ability. She later realized that his positive response and excitement about her work stimulated her desire and dream to have a career in his field.

A MENTOR GIVES
UPWARD MOBILITY TO CAREER

As previously stated, the greatest thing that a mentor does is to provide upward mobility to your career. Without this, there would be almost no tangible results of the value of a mentoring relationship. This is provided in a variety of ways. By speaking well of you to your superiors and by giving you exposure throughout the organization, you get both access to information and an introduction to people that you would not ordinarily have. Mentors can also assist in helping you early on design firm, clear, realistic goals and a program of career strategy and development. Successful mentoring can help you get a higher salary. Many women are seriously hampered by lesser wages and a lack of financial resources in general. Mentors can help rectify this and assist you in strategy for negotiating a salary they *know* is equal in the male world.

Mentors are often in the position to give extra responsibility. If they are not in your chain of command, they can invite you to assist on one of their projects. This can lead to increased visibility on your own job, and you can accomplish the job without going through stifling channels. This benefit is crucial as more women enter the work force in formerly male-dominated positions, and on occasion, mentors take key people with them as they move up. Mentorees may be taken if they make their mentor look good, complement their style, and if they work well together.

In *Men and Women of the Corporation*, Rosabeth Moss Kanter noted that by and large, mentors can determine who gets ahead. She states, "sponsored mobility seems to determine who gets the most desirable jobs."[1] To emphasize her belief that sponsors are absolutely essential for women, she made another interesting point: It is much harder for women (than men) to get the right mentor.

A MENTOR BOOSTS SELF-ESTEEM BY BELIEVING IN YOU

Another thing that mentors do is to boost your self-esteem by believing in you. This in itself can give renewed confidence. If someone you admire so much has faith that you can do the particular task, then maybe you can. Certainly you will do your utmost not to let your mentor down.

[1]Rosabeth Moss Kanter, *Men and Women of the Corporation* (New York: Basic Books, Inc., 1977), p. 181.

If the approval of your mentor is spread around the organization, others (both higher and on your level) will be influenced by it. The mentor can provide the final "stamp of approval" that enables you to gain the respect of others you hardly know. This endorsement can provide invitations to meetings and even social functions which say in effect, "you belong." It can also give a feeling of great security.

Mentors can be an especially great source of comfort during a crisis or turning point. Their continuing faith can often provide the extra push needed to renew your self-esteem and give the courage needed for success. Ruth Halcomb in *Across the Board* (the Conference Board's publication), states that: "Individuals seem to need mentors most at crisis periods or turning points in their careers."[2] Success or failure at such times greatly depends upon whether or not a mentor is present.

A MENTOR SHARES YOUR DREAMS

A mentor can also share your dreams. Daniel J. Levinson, who wrote *The Seasons of a Man's Life*, says the most crucial function of the true mentor is to "foster the young adult's development by believing in him (her), sharing the youthful Dream, giving it his blessing, helping to define the newly emerging self in its newly discovered world, and creating a space in which the young person can work on a reasonable satisfactory life structure that contains The Dream."[3] I don't know how many of you have had a dream and someone to share it with, but it can make all the difference if a mentor-figure believes that your dream is worthwhile. He can help you map out a plan of action and assist you in making your plan come true.

A MENTOR GIVES VISION

I would go a step beyond Levinson and say that a mentor also gives you vision, teaches you to "think big," and expands your horizons. His own

[2]Ruth Halcomb, "Mentors and the Successful Woman," *Across the Board,* February 1980, p. 13.
[3]Daniel J. Levinson, *The Season's of a Man's Life* (New York: Alfred A. Knopf, 1978), p. 99.

intellectual standards and curiosity can stimulate yours. A mentor can share his dream, goals, and insights in life and thus cause you to set your standards and hopes even higher, a function that can make a big difference in later life as well as in the present. The far-reaching effects of having your personal philosophy shaped by a mentor held in such high esteem is almost immeasurable. Once you learn to "think big," you never lose this perspective. Many professional people never learn this, and thus have very narrow vision, which is especially unfortunate in mid-level and above positions. These people are very difficult to work for, and certainly their contribution in any creative field is at a minimum.

A MENTOR PROVIDES ADVICE, COUNSEL, AND SUPPORT

MORAL SUPPORT IN A CRISIS   Giving advice, counsel, and support is another very valuable function that a mentor provides. Particularly in times of stress, a mentor is someone to turn to, a "port in the storm." Many women in my research commented at length that their mentor was especially valuable when they were in the middle of a career crisis, and that their mentor's support enabled them to hold their head up and survive many a near disaster with their pride at least partially intact.

ADVICE ON NEW POSITIONS   Of almost equal importance, a mentor can give advice on taking or not taking a new position, and what paths lead to blind alleys. So often women do not know what expertise is necessary for what jobs because they have not yet significantly experienced top positions. Sometimes men are the only ones who can provide this information for us.

However, when you ask your mentor for advice, more often than not you need to carry out the moves suggested by him. As a protegée, you have an implicit obligation to inform the mentor of your actions, especially if they are contrary to his advice. In this case, it is necessary to reassure him that his input was valuable, and let him know why different action was taken.

A MENTOR INTRODUCES YOU TO THE CORPORATE STRUCTURE, ITS POLITICS AND PLAYERS

A mentor can save you valuable time by introducing you to the corporate structure, its politics, and in teaching you to speak the language of that particular company. In short, he can let you know what is going on and help you to be part of it. He can also comment on the idiosyncrasies of the "players"; he can tell you which types to trust and which types are out to "get you." He can sometimes tell you when to fight for a particular idea and when not to. He can share the philosophy and values of the company and those running it. He can give advice on which contacts to develop and how to use them, and he can support your work to others at higher levels.

The mentor's "know-how" can also be valuable in writing memos or making presentations to unfamiliar groups higher up. Mentors develop leaders that will be the next "generation" to take over the corporation. They can use their influence to facilitate entry into committees that will be prestigious and will have the endorsement of the Chief Executive Officer. Mentors can also teach you who the heroes of the organization are. These are different from the power people (although they may have had power at one time). It is important to know who the heroes are and not to offend them!

Mentors can, when appropriate, begin to tear down social barriers and help stamp out discrimination. Women have been excluded from certain social dining facilities, or clubs, since the end of the seventeenth century when such exclusive "men only" clubs began to be highly popular in England. At such clubs, men engaged in business and politics without the interference of those "overgrown children" that Lord Chesterfield held women to be. Women who are struggling to be accepted in the establishment are at a severe disadvantage by not being able to carry on business in these informal settings. Mentors can petition for women to be included, while selecting other central dining places to invite "the establishment" to eat with their mentorees.

A MENTOR TEACHES BY EXAMPLE

A mentor can also teach just by his example. In some ways a mentoree can want to emulate his behavior much like a role model. Although it was noted earlier that a mentor can serve as a role model, a role model is never a mentor due to the lack of personal involvement. This is an important distinction. If the mentor is prestigious in the organization, you should take special note of his conduct in meetings, how he presents himself, who he connects with, and where his ideas are adopted. Mentors can also teach a social code of behavior and dress as well as an organizational one.

Many women in my studies echoed: "For years after my formal tutelage ended, I could solve certain problems by saying, 'How would my mentor have done this?'" Or, "How would he act in a particular situation?" Then the answer often becomes clear. Because we share our mentors' experiences and backgrounds, we often become a mirror image of their thoughts and performance. But, of course, if you are not on the same level, even though you are able to anticipate his response, you need to be aware that your ideas and actions may not get the same reception due to your position in the organization. Unfortunately for the junior, the lower one is in the company, the less likely one is of seeing his proposal, no matter how good, actually carried out.

A MENTOR IMPARTS VALUABLE INFORMATION

Another important function that the mentor provides is to keep the mentoree supplied with "inside" information that is not readily available. People learn at different rates and at different times. What your mentor has been telling you over and over again may suddenly sink in, as if you were hearing it for the first time.

Your mentor can tell you how your superior would react to a particular idea. He can also tell if your idea has been tried (and, most importantly, failed) and under what circumstances. If he knows you can keep his confidentiality, he will continue to keep you abreast; this information, which you could not get otherwise, can be useful indeed. It cannot be overemphasized enough that you must keep his trust. Of crucial importance, if you are lucky, some time in your career you may be secretly warned of a poteniallly dangerous situation. Being prepared may enable you to position yourself and gather your allies so that you can walk away unscarred before your career is harmed.

A MENTOR GIVES FEEDBACK
ON YOUR PROGRESS

How Do Others See You? A mentor is one person you can trust to give feedback on both your progress and how others view you. This can also include reality testing: Will your ideas fly in your organization? These frank conversations are infinitely more valuable than formal annual or even semi-annual performance appraisals. The mentor can say: "You do not relate well to your peers"; or "You need to be less aggressive." He can even give feedback on such mundane things as wardrobe, the pitch of your voice, or the fact that you need to take a public speaking course. These minor matters may seem unimportant to the beginning career woman, but they can keep you from being accepted by the establishment.

Modify Your Style Early in one's career, there is the opportunity to be aware of and modify one's style, if necessary. This style will have direct effect on how one plays office politics in later years. This is sometimes awkward for a boss to do, as his career can be affected, and thus he may be reluctant to be completely open. However, your mentor has nothing to lose, and you can have a two-way flow of information with complete confidence. This critique can be one of the most valuable aspects of the mentor relationship.

As Emerson said: "Our chief want in life is somebody who shall make us do what we can." Mentors do this well.

CASES

These three cases of Nancy, Diane, and Virginia illustrate some of the many significant things that mentors did for their careers.

Nancy K. Phillips
MIS Manager
Fairchild Optoelectronics Division

"I have been with Fairchild for two-and-a-half years and was previously with Fireman's Fund Insurance Company in San Rafael.

"My mentor's name is Richard Smith, and he came to Fairchild as director of data processing. I had been there about six months when he arrived, and the mentor relationship developed after I ended up working directly for him. Our age difference is fifteen years; I am thirty-three and he is in his late forties.

I liked Rich as a a person and found him to be very demanding and very particular; he was a challenge to work with. By demanding I mean that he was looking for quality and a high level of work. In the end he rewarded my efforts. He did not claim my work as his own but gave me credit, and he let upper management know that it was my work.

"Fairchild was later acquired by Schlumberger, and our group began decentralizing and breaking up the central data processing function in 1980. Rich was very good about letting the different general managers know about my skills and what I had done. My career most definitely would not have gone as far if he had not been there. He took a chance in backing me and in giving me different opportunities. He told me he was taking a risk in putting me out with others even more qualified to take over division data processing groups. He said what did not show on my resume was my willingness to work, to get things done, and my positive attitude. He thought I could do the job, even though I did not look heavily qualified on paper. I would not have let him down for anything—we supported each other.

"I was in favor of Rich's philosophies throughout this decentralization process, and this in turn helped his career. Other managers were not as willing to support him, but he knew he could count on me. He could tell me things in confidence, and often I was the only one who knew what was going on. He may have had other mentorees, but I know of only one other person (a man).

"Now Rich continues to support me, even though I no longer work in his organization. I am in the middle of the relationship and expect that it will continue on into the future. In turn, I try to help my staff develop as much as possible because I feel it is the responsibility of a good manager. As I continue in data processing, I think Rich will be an ally well into the future.

"The most significant thing Rich did for my career, or could ever do, was to allow me to interview and be accepted as an MIS manager. This elevated my position to where the choices available are infinitely greater than the ones I could have had in my previous position. It has set up my career just beautifully, and I could not have gotten this far without him. The new job is working out fine, and my management is very pleased. (No one looks at me and says: "I know how she got there.") Out of the twelve new MIS managers in the divisions, four are women, Fairchild has traditionally been good to women. When I joined the company, women were already in high-level management positions.

"I feel that the mentor relationship is a very positive one. When I started working after college, I had no idea that relationships like this could be so important or could do so much for a person's career. In fact, I didn't even know that they existed. I just assumed that my hard work would automatically be recognized and rewarded. This has really been a learning process for me. In college I knew I would work, but I had no idea where I would end up or what my goals were. It was not until I was about 27 that I actually started planning a career.

"My advice to younger women coming along would be to seek out this relationship. I have no doubt that the mentor relationship made a significant difference in my career. It has literally 'set up' the next ten years of my career, and I could not have done that on my own!"

Diane L. Young
Training and Development Officer
Southern Pacific Transportation Company

"I have had several mentors, all men, and the most significant was David Stevens of Bechtel's Training and Development Department. There is a difference of twenty years in our ages. David was not my boss, but someone I worked with who held a position much superior to mine. He was very helpful to me in a number of ways, but specifically in the area of training technology. As training was new to me, I had to educate myself in order to do the job. David has a Ph.D. in psychology and continually assessed where I was, what I needed, and made himself available to me. He encouraged me and answered my questions and didn't make me feel foolish or afraid to inquire further.

"For four years David encouraged me to explore and was delighted with some of the things I did on my own. I was always jumping into projects and making things happen. When he asked my advice about projects he was working on and bounced ideas off me, I really felt helpful to him.

I left Bechtel because I did not feel that they were serious about training and I wanted to find out if *I* was. David and I talked about this, and he felt my creativity would be stifled and I would burn out if I stayed.

"Now our working relationship has ended, but our friendship has not. We still call each other and talk about training issues. We talk about what we are working on, prospects for consulting, and we trade thoughts and materials. While our corporate climates are different, we can still trade ideas back and forth.

"I have also had other mentors, and they seem to live vicariously through me. As I was always into something new, they took a risk in backing me. In this way they could share in success and avoid responsibility for failure. Some of their common characteristics were that they were male, highly placed, happy to sponsor me, and their doors were always open. Most of my mentors have singled me out for highly visible projects—to prepare speeches and special programs. They've asked me to work on things that they've wanted 'done right the first time,' and have asked me to represent both them and the company in special projects. It is a nice feeling for them to have faith in my abilities. I work hard to live up to it!

"I believe I've helped my mentors' careers in other ways—I entertain them! I think they have a feeling of accomplishment. Most managers get things done through other people. They gain from this kind of relationship—because it looks good for them to have successful people under them.

"I grew up in a structured and disciplined atmosphere in which my character was formed by testing those barriers and limits. If this forms the foundation of my assertiveness (aggressiveness), then I guess it's also helped me in my organizational life. Barriers and limitations are for testing, questioning, and revising. Mentors may not be in a political position to do this. They can do it in a nonthreatening way through me.

"Working closely together strengthens a bond between you and your mentor. I think you have to be friends first, at least to the extent that you can criticize constructively. It is helpful to be told you are lacking in a certain area. The mentor bond is not only a business relationship but also a social one. You need to be able to rant and rave but also to share solitude with a mentor. The mentor needs to know what you are going through and be able to relate to you. I still have contact with and, in some cases,know the wives and children of my mentors.

"I have never had a conflict with a mentor. I know they will always be there for me, and I hope they know I will always be there for them. Without mentors, my career would definitely have been different. I do not believe women know this, otherwise they would make a conscious effort to find mentors, someone who will 'tell it like it is.' Mentors will tell you if you are going in the wrong direction, and often can give you some guidance before you 'fall on your face.'

"The biggest turning point in any mentor relationship is the amount of risk that anyone is willing to take on you. This depends on your confidence and attitude about yourself. If you believe in yourself, others will believe in you also. I think I'm great — I think I'm very good at what I do. I try to give it my best shot, and I work very, very hard. I am a risk taker and have given up on trying to please everyone all the time. To disappoint someone, or realize that everyone doesn't like me, is hard to cope with, but women especially need to be able to deal with this. It's a fact of life.

"I make time for women who need career counseling or help in putting together a resume, but I have not yet been a mentor. If a woman is interested in becoming involved in a mentor relationship, she has to make it happen. Almost anyone will be your mentor if you really want them to be, but *you must make the original contact.* Go after it! Have some thoughts prepared before you get there and tell them: 'I have thought about this. Can you give me directions, and can I check back with you?' It is up to you to single out a mentor. If you wait for it to happen, it won't. Potential mentors are likely to be busy people, so you must approach them.

"If the would-be mentor is up at the top, you will be surprised how really pleased they are that someone is asking for their direction and ideas. Take the initiative, but be prepared to do your part and don't expect someone to hand you anything. It is hard work! Like a contract, there are duties and responsibilities that must be complied with. You can't just 'take, take, take.' You have to give something to the relationship. You will need to inform the mentor on how things are going and what you have uncovered. Be ready to hold up your end of the bargain.

"I can't emphasize the social aspects enough. It is good to have a nonoffice relationship. You cannot separate the business, social, emotional, and spiritual aspects—you are one person. If you can, try to get away occasionally from the business atmosphere with your mentor, if only for lunch. It has to be give-and-take, a two-way street. They, too, need to have some benefit if the relationship is to continue."

Virginia F. Hess
Contract Negotiator
Electric Power Reseach Insitute

"My mentor, Adam Wilson, employed me at perhaps the low point of my life. I had moved around for six years with my husband, who was first a naval officer and then became an engineer in a small town. Our move to California was predicated on my wish to develop a career as well as on my husband's decision to go back to school for an M.B.A. It took me four months at the end of the 1974 recession to find a job. Adam believed in me enough to hire me and then bolstered my self-esteem by complimenting my work.

"Because we communicated so well, specific feedback was essential. I could tell from his expression as he read a memo what his reaction would be. His positive response to my work, and the excitement about it, stimulated my desire to have a career in that field. Adam was very sensitive to the fact that he had been given a chance by *his* employer, and he knew that by giving me a chance he would get loyalty, dedication, and good work. His belief in my ability was a prime motivator for me. The other motivation was the chance of promotion. I have held five jobs in the five years I have been in this field, and each time I was promoted.

"At the time I was hired, I was changing careers. Adam was happy to find someone applying for an entry-level position who had a fairly high level of education and was a bit more mature than someone just out of college. What did he do for my career? He talked me into specializing in contracts work. After five years I am not sure that I should have spent this much time in this area, but I can certainly work anywhere now in contracts. At times, he actively sponsored me, exposing my work to higher management and counseling me how to structure my responses to their questions. He told me he intended to be my mentor; he used the word 'mentor.' He said when he finished Stanford he was hired and given a chance when he really knew nothing at all about business. He was told by his first mentor that the only requirement for such help was to pass on his kind of deeds to someone else. So Adam consciously chose to become my mentor, and I was the first person that he chose at EPRI. He has since actively been a mentor to other people. Now I feel a responsbility to mentor others. I am at the highest level of any woman in my department, and there are about fifteen women under me waiting for me to leave so that they can have a chance to be promoted.

"When I first went to work for Adam, if he liked a report I had written, he gave me full credit and made sure that I was allowed to take it to his boss. That was important to me because, through Adam, I was able to meet some of the higher management. I appreciated his straightforward attitude. He also drew organization charts on the blackboard and said: 'This is where I think you can go in the company.' Because he helped structure the department he used the opportunity to create growth opportunities for its members. Knowing that a promotion was possible if I performed well, I worked very, very hard. It was a great incentive! I could compare Adam to a beneficent Machiavelli. Specifically, he gave me the opportunity to do good work; he let me do negotiations with the big firms and 'walked me through' beforehand. He could have given them to more experienced persons. He gave me his time and, salary-wise, he had my job reclassified. I now make three times what I made when I went to work five years ago.

"For my mentor's career, I was a very good employee. I was dedicated, eager, did good work, and made him look good. That was one of the things that you are supposed to do for your boss. He has been consistently promoted over the past five years, and I think it is because he has the reputation for building a good team. You can't go onto the next job until you have a good replacement, and he has managed always to train a good team.

"In many ways, the mentor relationship has ended, mainly because of my feelings of salary discrimination. As the highest ranking woman in the department, I was always paid less than all the professional men, partly because I was hired initially at so low a wage. Finally, last year the department hired two men below me (one of whom was my replacement) and paid both of them more than they were paying me in my new job—and I was supposed to train them! I went through the roof.

"At the time, I was not in a good position to complain formally or to hunt for a new position because I was pregnant and planning on a six-month leave of absense. Soon after I announced I was pregnant, the department came through with a technical adjustment for me which incidentally put me ahead of the two younger men. But harsh words had been spoken on both sides. I see this as a classic salary compensation problem—not being paid for 'equal work' because of a low starting salary. The problem was compounded by my being promoted frequently in the same company. In order for the company to hire anyone from the outside, they would have had to pay a much higher salary than I am getting. Of course the department felt that I should be grateful for the rapid promotion and not worry so much over salary!

"So I went off on six months leave of absence, and later I wrote Adam a note inviting him to come by and see the new baby, which he did. I thought it would be difficult to look for a new job coming off a maternity leave, and I am now in the position of figuring out whether I can continue to stay in this job and work for him—and see if he bears a grudge. I think Adam might. My boss says he doesn't, my friends say he doesn't, but I know him very well, and I am unsure.

"I also have to prove myself again to be a trusted member of the team. I was formerly seen as not subversive in any way, and then I accused management of being discriminatory. This was difficult to handle for a boss who actively promoted women in his organization.

"However, the salary disparity still exists between my pay and that of the male negotiators. The department finally hired another woman negotiator, and I think her salary is even less than mine. So the two women are paid less than all the men for the same work. My management would like me to believe it is a question of experience, but in my field experience is hard to quantify.

"It is hard to forecast my future relationship with my mentor. I am constantly trying to figure this out, and I want to stay good professional friends. I need to give Adam the credit for moving into a tough situation himself, because he is the youngest division director by about twenty years. Most of the directors are utility executives who have come to EPRI to cap their already successful careers. Someday I would like to talk to Adam about what he thinks it means to be a mentor, and whether or not he feels he is an ex-mentor at this point. I think he has found it very dangerous to get so wrapped up in people, because I see a very definite conflict between a mentor's desires for his pupil and his managerial responsibilities. If you work closely together, sooner or later you are going to have this conflict. Hopefully it can be resolved, or at least the two people can part with mutual respect."

"For these reasons, one of my lessons for younger women is never to choose your boss as your mentor so that neither career nor job responsibilities are affected by the mentor relationship. I know I would never be at this level today if it weren't for Adam's backing me.

"I have not had other mentors in my career, but right now I don't feel a need for this kind of relationship. Adam taught me that I can go to management for advice without fear of it reflecting poorly on my professional competence. I feel very comfortable with management and grateful that my mentor taught me a philosophy of 'no surprises.'"

CHAPTER THREE

Selecting a Mentor

Selected by her mentor as someone with great potential, Betty was asked to be on the program committee of the San Francisco Section AIAA. Later, when she was elected section chairman of the AIAA, the third largest engineering professional organization in the country, she well realized the importance of that relationship.

After not having a mentor for a year, Audrey decided to seek a mentor. She started by selecting some very high executives and asking their advice. Later, she settled on one who thought her work was excellent; he made her feel supported and challenged.

The relationship began when Toni's mentor, the Chairman of the Board, sought her out of her Stanford MBA class and asked, "Are you coming with us?" He took a personal interest in her from then on; when she later left the company to start her own consulting firm, he was one of her first clients.

HOW DO YOU SELECT A MENTOR?

Most women do not know the rules about selecting a mentor. Men, on the other hand, are much more sophisticated. Betty Harragan, author of *Games Mother Never Taught You,* emphasizes that not only are we not playing with the Big Boys, but we don't know what games they are playing. She repeatedly says that until we do, we won't be accepted. We should not try to change the rules, she says, but simply try to join the game! Women are slow to learn that the game of work has its own rules and customs, not only set up by men but controlled by men. One game is the mentor game, and we need to understand it as the men do. In discussing the invasion of women in the corporate hierarchy, Harragan states: "Understandably, most of them are totally unprepared for the situations they will encounter. Worse yet, the vast majority are oblivious to the fact that they have stumbled onto a playing field where the rules of participation are rigidly enforced and the criteria for success are known to all but them."[1]

Women often wait to be selected by a prospective mentor, do not have their eyes open, and are not as aggressive or even as "calculating" as they should be. There are, of course, exceptions as women reach the top echelons of management. Then they know and play the game as well as their male counterparts. Their only problem is trying to find players who are receptive to letting them in the game.

What is absolutely important is for you to *know* you want to be developed. You must know you need special coaching or grooming, and be willing to learn for this kind of relationship to develop. Be willing to admit you don't know everything about certain areas. It is also important not to get caught up in a mentor's style that is not your own. It is necessary to be yourself. You can observe someone else's pattern, but you need to be comfortable in developing your own style against their framework.

AIM FOR THE STARS   While it is true that the mentor relationship is a "two-way street," there is often a choice of who has potential to become one's mentor. Aim for the stars! If, of course, you can get the CEO (Chief Executive Officer), Academic Dean, or head of your professional department to be your mentor, you will have it made; unfortunately, the majority cannot do this.

[1]Betty Lehan Harragan, *Games Mother Never Taught You* (New York: Warner Books, 1977), p. 23.

GO FOR THE POWER LINES   What is second best to having the number one as your mentor? Mentors need to be chosen who are close to the power line. Does he have easy access to the top? Or access to those who do? Or at a minimum, access to the power in a lower division? You certainly would not want to choose someone who is out of favor with those higher up who can affect your career.

NEVER, NEVER SELECT YOUR BOSS   There are some general rules to follow: Women should never, never select their bosses. Mainly because you need a mentor with whom you can discuss your own boss, and your objective relationship with him, especially if there are personality conflicts. Although many of the cases in this book contradict this statement, they illustrate that women today do not know all the rules in selecting mentors. However, the cases also illustrate well that women are beginning to understand the logic and state themselves that one's mentor should not be one's immediate boss.

Second, you should not have a mentor that is even in your chain-of-command (i.e., your bosses' boss). And for the same reasons. A mentor should be someone who will not "gain or lose" because of (a) your decisions or work performance, and (b) whether or not you move by getting promoted within the same company or by changing to another company. However, the relationship between those on the same chain of command make it unlikely for a mentoring atmosphere. Reporting to someone makes the relationship susceptible to stress, competition, some jealousy, and often positioning for favors from the top, all opposite from the relationship you hope to find. Finding the right mentor can be tough, if not downright impossible, at times!

DO YOU SELECT YOUR MENTOR?

ADMIRATION/TRUST SHOULD OUTWEIGH INFERIORITY/ENVY   In selecting your mentor, you should try to choose someone for whom you feel admiration, affection, respect, trust, and even love in the broadest sense. These feelings should outweigh any negative emotions such as a feeling of lesser importance, envy, or being threatened. These feelings can be especially present in competitive women when someone outranks them.

A MENTOR IS NOT A HUSBAND   While I have chosen the words affection, admiration, and even love, I still need to clarify their use in the professional sense. The selection of a mentor is *not* similar and should not be confused with the selection of a husband. The mentor relationship is characterized by very distinct criteria. First, it is a temporary relationship; and second, it is not and should not be the primary emotional relationship in a woman's life (and it would be very unrealistic for her to think of it in this light). There are important criteria in the mentor relationship which are *not* transferable to the husband one, and vice versa.

Women in the past have sometimes been accused of having difficulty working with men in a professional capacity, of "falling in love" with their bosses, academic advisors, therapists, and others in leadership roles. The purpose of mentor selection is different. A husband presupposes a lengthy if not lifetime emotional commitment to one another's overall growth and to the growth of the relationship. You can adore your husband with an emotional commitment, but the level of professional adoration, reverence, and appreciation given to a mentor leaves you free to be an independent person. You are not bound to accept everything blindly, and thus you keep your perspective on the work situation.

One final word of advice. When you find the right mentor, you never actually say: "Will you be my mentor?" This is the number one rule of beginning the relationship (and it is certainly time for women to have some firm rules!). This would show both your lack of sophistication and a lack of organizational understanding. Mentor relationships take time to develop, and they develop gradually. During the early stages you can be verbally appreciative of extra help, attention, and assistance a potential mentor gives without actually asking for the mentor role. In fact, on looking back on mentor relationships, most mentorees cannot recall an exact time when they felt they had found their mentor. The relationship seems to begin when the mentor is both supportive and demanding, and the mentoree feels stretched and appreciated.

The danger in not finding a mentor is that one is liable to become too complacent...there is no one to push you, no one to take a risk for or, even more dramatic, no one to fail for!

Agnes Missirian at Bentley College, Massachusetts, surveyed *Business Week*'s top 100 business women on their "supportive professional relationships." She sent out 100 questionnaires and interviewed 15 of the women in depth. She concluded: "All of the highest-ranking corporate women in the country have had a mentor." And, with so few women in top and key positions, women know they will need all the help they can get. They must seek out, select, and widely use an influential and selfless mentor.

DOES YOUR MENTOR SELECT YOU?

QUALITIES WHICH ATTRACT PRESTIGIOUS MENTORS   Do the mentors select the mentorees, and if so, what qualities in younger workers attract prestigious mentors? Certainly mentors are not going to waste time with younger women who are not serious about getting ahead, or with those who fail to make a full commitment to their job and their organization. Mentors are attracted to dedication, enthusiasm, intelligence, and hard work. They gravitate to women who work well with others, who are willing to share information, and who seem to "catch on" to the corporate politics and fit the corporate image.

When you want to be "selected," get attention by publicizing your goals. Let it be known that you are willing to accept more responsibility, that you want to get ahead, and that you are willing to take risks to do so. Seek visibility by volunteering to be part of a new committee, and better yet, take a leadership role by offering to chair the new entity. If nothing else seems to work, offer to form a "task force" to look into what you consider a problem area. This is a sure way to get attention from upstairs, especially if you can think of a way to save the organization money! Become a technical master at your own job and maximize your opportunities. Look for "signals" from upstairs. Is there someone who likes your work and tells you so? Is this person a prospective mentor? With all this effort, someone is bound to need help with a new project at some point, remember you, and ask you to be of assistance.

WHAT MENTORS EXPECT IN RETURN   Mentors welcome having mentorees as disciples who will go forth and carry out their words of wisdom. It enhances the mentor's career to have under his protective wing several of the firm's brightest women who seem to be designed to move into the upper echelons. Does someone higher in the organization need help with an assignment? Volunteer! While it may take extra time weekends and evenings, it will be worth it in the long run. Try to get in a leadership position with high visibility. Someone higher up is bound to notice and want you on his team, especially if you let him know you are interested in what he is doing. If you are aggressive and bright, you should be able to develop a loyal group of established admirers.

This is how one of my mentors sums up his feeling of who selects whom: "I think that any mentor worth having would be too smart to let himself (or herself) be recruited by any cunning, manipulating, ambitious youngster. One doesn't acquire friends that way either. Perhaps the best advice to the high-potential youngster would be (1) do the job you've got the best you know how; (2) learn to listen, particularly to those whose breadth of experience exceeds yours; show appreciation to anyone who expresses an interest in how you're getting along; (3) if you think you see a better way to get the work done in terms of quality, time, or cost, suggest it to your boss; and (4) if an executive senior in rank to you gives you suggestions or opportunities relating to your career, be responsive and appreciate and still use your own best judgment. A 'mentor' relationship may develop or it may not; if it does, it will have its own 'life cycle.' Even the appearance of trying to 'use' or exploit someone's interest in you to serve your own ambitions will kill it. If the institution is a better place or does a better job because you're there, it's a fair certainty that you will have opportunities to rise in the ranks."

"CARE AND FEEDING" OF MENTORS

Once you are selected, you need to show your appreciation for your mentor's time and attention. Tell him often that you appreciate his interest and guidance. Keep him informed, and if you don't take his advice, be sure to discuss why.

The mentor relationship is a two-way street. Once your mentor has selected you, he also needs to gain from the relationship. What are some of the things you can do for his career? You can share your accomplishments; implement his ideas and projects; support him with your colleagues, both vocally and by your actions; give him your honest opinion when he asks for it (which can be a fresh perspective); work hard to make him look good; and value the relationship.

Once you are selected, I believe it is a good idea to keep your mentor informed in general on your personal life as well as your professional one. But do omit the smaller details! Often the largest hurdle yet to be resolved for women is their responsibilities at home. Tell him briefly about your children and your husband, as well as additional obligations you may have to other family members, community activities, boards and committees. This will *not* make you seem less dedicated to your career. Chances are, due to your mentor's higher visibility, you know a lot more about him. It never hurts to give him a glimpse of that "other side" of you, and let him know what other demands you are balancing. You may also want to add that you are quite capable of juggling it all!

While it is true that men probably never do this, women are not yet as free of outside responsibilities. With the double standard, the major part of the home and childcare still falls on the female; my experience as a single parent raising three sons taught me it was an excellent idea to keep my mentor updated. Most professional women are well organized enough to cope with minor home emergencies and remain on the job, but for those rare occasions, I believe it can only be in your best interest to inform your mentor, as well as your boss, about your home life, so that they will be understanding and supportive in an unusual crisis.

CASES

The following cases point out how Betty and Toni were selected by their mentors, and how Audrey fared in trying to select hers.

Betty K. Berkstresser
Technical Assistant to the Chief
Helicopter and Powered Lift Technology Division
NASA/Ames Research Center

"My mentor was Warren Randall, then a senior engineer at NASA Ames. I came to NASA Ames in 1971 as an aerospace engineer in the Mission Analysis Division. In this office I had good visibility and an opportunity to see programs from a Center perspective. Our relationship began about six years ago when Warren asked me to be on the program committee of the San Francisco Section of the American Institute of Aeronautics and Astronautics (AIAA). Warren was the current program director and expected to be elected an officer; he was subsequently elected treasurer, secretary, vice-chairman, and chairman. There is about twenty years difference in our ages; I am 35 and he is around 55. Warren saw me as someone who had potential, and he wanted to make sure that I had the benefit of his experiences.

"I was later sent to NASA headquarters in Washington for a year in a training program, and on my return the San Francisco section chairman asked me to be regional affairs director. As a result of being a director for one year, I was interested in this position. I was asked to be program director the next year, then the nominating committee nominated me for treasurer. Nationally there are about 25,000 members, and about 1,500 in the San Francisco section. We are about the third largest engineering professional organization in the country but, unfortunately, only about 5 percent of the members are women. I was subsequently elected treasurer, secretary, vice-chairman and chairman (although one person wrote on his ballot that he was not yet ready for a woman as chair!). I received tremendous support not only from Warren but also from the members. Their applause at the end of my introductions was almost electrifying.

"I would call my relationship with Warren a classic mentor relationship. Warren arranged for me to be appointed a director which, of course, lead to my being the chair. He was constantly by my side, always calling, always helping, checking in, making suggestions, adding something. He certainly had picked me; there was no doubt of this.

"As to my background, my father was a civil engineer, and I became interested in engineering through him. I had all the typical problems going through engineering school that you might expect. The younger women today are not facing them as we did. When I was in college, women were discouraged from majoring in engineering. I started work with NASA in Houston during my junior year as a cooperative education student. This was a program where the student would work for a semester and go to school for a semester. When I graduated, NASA made me the best offer. I had the unspoken doubt — 'can she make it?' — follow me all the way through engineering school. I feel that women have to work harder and shine brighter to be accepted.

"The AIAA experience has given me tremendous visibility and has allowed managers to see me in action. However, I am not sure that my success as chair of the San Francisco Section AIAA has followed over to my career; but hopefully the men will be comfortable with my leadership, and this experience will begin to accelerate my career. I also think it is time for me to seek a mentor who will be instrumental in my upward mobility.

"I have not had other mentors besides Warren, but there have been role models—men that I picked to learn from, but no one else has selected me. These men chose to be very professional and very distant. Since I became chair, Warren now treats me as a peer. I occasionally ask his advice, but in some ways I believe I have passed Warren. He is now assistant branch chief at NASA Ames, and apparently content to remain at the branch level of management. Warren is a very unassuming although very sensitive person, and I think our relationship is typical of those that have leveled out. We talk occasionally and see each other at meetings about twice a month.

"If I had a problem, I would still go to him. He is sufficiently removed from my line of management that I can talk about the personalities with whom I am currently involved. He has not encouraged me to look ahead to a Center Director position or similarly higher one, but he had encouraged me to be a mentor to younger engineers. In return, I believe Warren wanted to have been a factor in the development of future managers. I never had the feeling that Warren was helpful because I was a woman; as far as I can tell, he treated the women he sponsored the same as the men.

"Warren is the only male in a family which includes two daughters. There is the possibility that he saw me as a 'daughter' who wanted to follow in his footsteps—I don't know. Warren liked to bounce ideas off me, and he had a lot of trust in me. These things gave me confidence in myself and made me grow. I would not have been exposed to decision-making at a high level as early if Warren had not given me this opportunity. I also believe I made Warren stand out and I gave him a certain 'pizzaz.'

"Now I am a mentor to both women and men engineers. I have appointed, cajoled, and pushed a lot of women to AIAA committees, which I could do as the chair. This is a terrific opportunity for the women, for as they work with men, they begin to understand what their role is as a team member, and what they must be to compete professionally. It is a good opportunity for men as well to see how capable women work. Sometimes women don't get the exposure unless they are almost forced into it. I try to treat the young men and women the same, but I may be more supportive and patient with the women.

"This impatience with men surfaced recently when I was in charge of a 'Fly-in' for the AIAA's fiftieth anniversary celebration. I picked a young engineer from my group to head it up because he is a person who pumps your hand and seems 'up and coming.' He turned out to be more talk than work. A second young engineer I picked to be regional affairs director was just great; everything a director should be: details, plans, follow-up letters, and calls to keep me informed.

"Later, a woman aerospace education specialist I picked to be newsletter editor performed so well that the AIAA nominating committee nominated her for treasurer. She is now on her way up the ladder, and I am pleased I had a hand in it. In a volunteer organization, you appeal to the members' professionalism because you don't supervise them in a salaried situation.

"Concerning sex, I don't think Warren Randall ever even winked at me! This was delightful. I never had to worry that if I were too friendly he might take it the wrong way. This can be a problem for career women. I don't believe men can mentor well if there is a sexual relationship. I suppose sexual overtones are bound to come up because the mentor relationship is a close one, but to act on them would make the relationship change, and not for the better. So my advice to younger women is not to risk it; it won't help your career in the long run."

Audrey Wells
Manager, Product Planning
Syntex (USA), Inc.

"I had not had a mentor for a year when I decided to seek one. I went to some very high-level executives to seek their advice on where I should be going careerwise. They were very cordial and helpful at this time, but none seemed appropriate for a mentor relationship. I have learned that no matter how much one values the mentor relationship, you cannot always have it when you want or need it. You probably have a better chance of finding such a relationship if you are open and receptive, but this alone does not guarantee that you will be able to locate a mentor.

"Then a new man appeared on the scene, and he has become a mentor of a sort. He is very supportive of me, gives me lots of autonomy, is easy to work with, has an open style, and provides the resources with which to work. He thinks my work is excellent (up to the standards of the *Harvard Business Review*). I need lots of freedom and open communication. He recognized and supported my needs, and we work well together.

"Looking back on earlier mentor relationships, I realize that my most important one occurred at the start of my business career. I met my most influential mentor, John Williams, at Syntex when I first applied for a position. He was then the director of marketing research and was ready to hire a woman in a management position. He was sensitized to seeing women in roles other than the traditional wife and mother. I wanted to make a change from academia to business and had been distributing my resume to different companies. My first mentor was actually younger than me by about two or three years and was very interested in my academic credentials. He saw that I had background characteristics that could fit the job, and although I was not interested at first, he sold me on the job and I took it.

"The mentor situation began developing when I realized that John had taken a risk in hiring me. There were sixty male marketing managers and I was the first woman. I was asked by the vice president of marketing if I realized there was travel and commitment (since I had a husband and small child). I told him I had demonstrated my career commitment when I got my Ph.D. while raising a small child, and not to worry. This issue was never raised again.

"John guided me, talked in terms of giving me visibility, and discussed the development of my writing skills. He continued to talk about my career, my ultimate goal and what steps would be necessary to get there. I was not used to thinking in these terms and at first felt awkward during these discussions. He talked in terms of a bigger view and asked me to think about and plan my career within a larger framework. I was pleasantly surprised, especially since I came from academia where I had to fight for everything I wanted. I loved the department and the relationship with my new boss.

"He gave me all the authority, resources, and freedom I needed. For example, he sent me to courses and provided me with tutors to allow me to acquire the financial background I lacked. I did not have to struggle to get access to needed information. John provided me with a tape recorder for field interviews and sent me to Princeton to interview an expert at my request. He freed me to realize my potential.

"This was a critical period. At that time there were only male managers in the Syntex research labs, sales force, and marketing department. Although the majority were supportive, there were a few who wanted me to 'go away.' Their wives were at home with small children, and they didn't want them to try to match my career. I also had problems with several women employees who felt threatened by my having a Ph.D., being attractive, having a happy marriage, and on top of this, managing a small child. They questioned how they could compete with me. Fortunately, I could discuss all this with my mentor.

"My relationship with my mentor was very open and honest, and we were continuously striving to integrate me into the organization. He felt that if I was going to be successful, I would have to get along with even the few who didn't welcome my presence. He helped me to understand the personality differences of the various managers and over time provided feedback which was very helpful in learning how to handle their egos and help *them* to make the adjustment to accepting a woman as a peer. We developed a common view that I should do the job the best I could and when I received accolades from higher-ups, the rank-and-file would fall into place. This is just what eventually happened. I received a commendatory memo from the president on a project I completed, and all the petty problems disappeared. I was finally accepted as 'one of the guys.'

"After only a year and a half in my new position, I was approached to consider a promotion to a different department. I was very surprised and flattered, yet felt challenged and content in my current position. So I questioned whether the time was right for a change. My mentor took me to a lovely French restaurant for lunch and gave me all the time I needed to discuss the position as well as the pros and cons of changing jobs at that time. He provided crucial advice and counsel, and stated that the promotion was an excellent opportunity for me. He also told me: 'I know you don't feel ready yet for this job, but if at any time you want to come back, the door is always open. I am right there behind you. You may not have as much visibility in this new job, but you will be forced to grow.'

"Later he was at upper level meetings at which I participated, and gave me feedback on how I was perceived in my new position. Once again, I was the first woman in the position and, at this time, in the whole industry as well, so it wasn't surprising that there were new interpersonal frictions again. My mentor guided me in this new broader group of contacts which included the field sales force.

"At a later time, when considering a change from a line to a staff position, I telephoned my mentor, who had transferred to another division, to discuss the change. I felt that I needed opportunities to learn new areas. I would have the chance to speak several foreign languages I learned in Europe as a student, and also to travel internationally. My plan was to take the new position and acquire additional training, which would well prepare me to return later in an even higher position. A breaking point in my mentor relationship occurred when I did not follow his advice in regard to this position. Perhaps the fact that he didn't know the people involved in the new area was another factor in the ending of the mentor relationship. Ever since this time, John has been more of a colleague and friend. We exchange Christmas letters and enjoy seeing each other when he is in town, but the mentor relationship ended at this point.

"Today I have assumed the mentor role to women and even men are beginning to come to me for career counseling. I am currently counseling several women and find mentoring most gratifying when I see them move up and achieve their career goals.

"In summary, the most important thing my original mentor did for me was to have great confidence in me—more than I had in myself at that time. He saw so far ahead; he already saw me moving on a career path into a vice president level when all I wanted was an entry-level position. He told people: 'Audrey thinks I hired her because she is a woman; I hired her because she was far better qualified than the other candidates.'"

> *Toni Casey*
> Owner
> T. Casey's Inc.

"I worked for Saga Corporation during the summer between my first and second year at the Graduate School of Business at Stanford University. There I met my mentor, Lowell Davis, who was at that time chairman of the board and one of the founders. We were introduced when he took it on himself to meet all six of the summer M.B.A. students.

"After I graduated from Stanford I was trying to decide between Saga and another company. I saw Lowell at the GSB Arbuckle Award Dinner. He approached me and said: 'Are you coming with us?' I was very flattered that Lowell remembered me and knew who I was. Thus Lowell was very instrumental in my decision to accept their offer.

"I joined Saga's newly formed corporate development group, an internal consulting group, which reported directly to Lowell. My initial assignment was the leadership of a significant project for Saga's health care division, and Lowell was instrumental in obtaining this high level of responsibility for me.

"Throughout my career at Saga, Lowell took a personal interest in me. He watched my skills very closely, and he became very much aware of how competent I was in my ability to analyze and to write succinctly. He would have me edit or rewrite some of his work or the work of his executives. On occasion, he would then submit my work directly to the board of directors. Although I did not get credit for the work, Lowell knew that I had done it, and his opinion of me continued to grow. There was something that 'clicked' between us, a kind of chemistry that promotes trust, respect, and fun. We could laugh and even be silly at times.

"Sometimes I thought my close association with Lowell probably hurt me as much as helped me because the relationship caused resentment throughout the corporation. But in retrospect, I would not change anything. The total contribution that he made to my life is far greater than any difficulties that I encountered because of him.

"What Lowell did for my career was to help me gain a tremendous amount of confidence, to stand up for myself and my values, and to know that I could cope with the political situation in a corporation. As the highest level woman in my area, this was important.

"I worked at Saga for two-and-a-half years. During my time there, I was not as close to Lowell as I became after I left. At times I felt in awe of him, as he can be a very intimidating individual. It took me some time to get to where I understood him well enough so that I was not scared of him. I remember my first conflict with him. This occurred when I had been with the company for about two months. Saga had scheduled their annual executive meeting at a place called the Family Farm in Woodside, a private club. I, along with one other woman M.B.A., were the only women supposed to attend; however, the Family

Farm did not allow women on their premises. As you might expect, I was furious. I wrote a letter to Lowell the day that I heard that the other woman and I were going to be excluded.

"Luckily one of my Saga friends suggested that I sleep on the letter before mailing it. I rewrote it the next day in a far more positive way, and Lowell responded immediately. He called in the vice president of human resources and we had a series of early morning meetings. There were no other high-level females, but he called in other women confidantes. None of them believed that it was right to hold the meeting at a place where women could not attend! In the final analysis, the meeting was held at the Family Farm because of the tremendous effort it would have taken to notify everyone of a change and cancel the arrangements at that late a date. Although I 'lost the battle,' I felt I had 'won the war.' Saga will never have another meeting at the Family Farm but, more importantly, the issue of women's equality had been recognized and addressed. I believe the whole incident was the real beginning of my mentor relationship with Lowell. I am sure that he admired my strength in the confrontation, and I certainly admired his ability and desire to listen.

"I left the company after I finished a major project in Washington, D.C. I ended up starting my own consulting business, and several Saga executives were my first clients, including Lowell. One project that I did for Lowell was to study the role of the board of directors and its functions. I attended a board of directors seminar at Columbia University in New York, which was attended primarily by presidents and chairmen. I learned a lot about board roles, and as a result wrote an article which was widely read at Saga and elsewhere.

"After a couple of years of consulting, I began developing a concept featuring a healthy fast food restaurant chain. When I actually decided to do it, Lowell became my unofficial board of advisors and was a tremendous help in the entire process. Not only because he supported me and thought my ideas were great, but also because he criticized me when I was off base or had not thoroughly thought out a particular aspect of the business. I could bounce ideas off him. I could share with him my fears and concerns. I learned a lot through my first venture and have recently expanded into a second unit with an even better location.

"One outstanding thing that Lowell did for me in my initial negotiations was to agree to guarantee my lease for the first restaurant.

Although it ended up not being necessary, it was a very significant thing for him to do and indicated his level of confidence in me. He has become a personal friend as well, and I also see him on social occasions.

"Lowell is very concerned about the human relations aspect of business. I have not met many executives like Lowell who believe in standards of the highest quality and excellence in customer service. He believes that if you take care of your employees and your customers, the profits will follow. This is a unique characteristic of Lowell, and one that I hope to pattern myself after. Lowell also personally handled any employee complaint that came to his office.

"In general, I feel that mentors are very valuable. It is like having parents; you need their direction and advice. What you get is the benefit of their mistakes and the knowledge of their experience. You don't have to learn everything the hard way and reinvent the wheel each time around. Mentors may not push you to the top, but they help you get there by not making you go through so many trials and errors. A good mentor provides enthusiasm and support and acts as a sounding board. They also make you feel good about yourself, give you encouragement when you are in doubt, and support you in times of adversity. There has to be a chemistry and an equal respect between two people for this kind of a relationship. I don't know how you find mentors, but they are very necessary.

CHAPTER FOUR

Can and Should You Have More Than One Mentor?

Sandra discovered that at different times in her career, two mentors were at pivotal points: one in the public arena and the other helping her to jump into the private sector. Later, she was constantly affirmed of the value of the two mentors, especially when they were specialists in two entirely different areas.

Joanne once had two mentors at the same time. While they were in different fields, both were instrumental in guiding her career. Later, she realized how each boosted her in a way the other did not, and that they were both equally powerful and important in her life for different reasons.

Mentors played an important role in Carole's career. She had one significant mentor and three less significant ones who helped her get where she is today. Later she said they paved the way for her in fields where few women were found.

MORE THAN ONE MENTOR AT A TIME

Although I personally do not feel that more than one mentor relationship is feasible at any one time, there are others who disagree. I feel that the relationship is too intense and takes too much commitment. Some say that it is almost like having more than one husband. However, a marital relationship presupposes a lifetime emotional commitment to each other's growth and to the growth of the relationship. The mentor relationship is temporary, and confined to one's work area.

With a good mentor relationship, you can simultaneously capitalize on other kinds of relationships: encouraging boss, helpful peers, role models, networks, and supportive professional groups. Networking relationships are especially important to a woman serious about getting ahead, as are professional women's conferences.

Researchers who disagree with me state that one should not have just one, but two or three mentors concurrently because, if your mentor loses power within the organization, you can move on with another. With the uncertainty of today's climate, often the "heir apparent" is passed over in favor of someone from outside the organization who can make a greater profit. If you can quickly detach yourself, you can move on and upward with another. Other researchers add that if you are related to a number of mentors, you will not get all your advice and views of the business filtered through a single person's perspective. I think the relationship is too personal and intense to shift mentors in a short period but, as in most issues, there are always two sides.

Gail Sheehy, author of *Passages*, wrote an article for *New York Magazine* in 1976 called, "The Mentor Connection: The Secret Link in the Successful Woman's Life." In this article, she stressed the importance of successful women having one or more mentors.[1]

MORE THAN ONE MENTOR DURING YOUR CAREER

Most men certainly experience more than one mentor relationship during their careers. In fact, most studies define a mentor as a "transitional figure." Women certainly should be able to do the same.

[1]Gail Sheehy, "The Mentor Connection: The Secret Link in the Successful Woman's Life," *New York Magazine*, April 5, 1976.

Mentor relationships are not designed to last the life of a working career and, as we are discovering, many factors contribute to the breakup. While a woman seldom is fortunate enough to step immediately into a new mentor relationship at the exact end of the old one, certainly she should have her eyes open for the next mentor opportunity. According to my research, most males experience three to four mentors. Although women should be able to do this, the data collected in my sample of 400 mentor questionnaires shows that it is closer to one to three.

If one has several mentors, the first mentor in a person's career may be particularly important. In very formative years, he can help set the stage for rapid growth and a mental frame of mind that confirms early on that you want a career, not just a position.

WHEN YOU DON'T NEED A MENTOR

WHEN YOU ARE CONTENT   I believe that there are two times in your career when you *don't* need a mentor. One time is when you are content with the status quo and do not want to move up, and this can happen in various stages of one's career. On rare occasions, you may feel your job is just right for you, and you don't want to change it in any way. Also, if one is involved with simultaneous challenges and rewards outside of the work place, one may not want more responsibilities on the job.

WHEN THE ORGANIZATIONAL CHART IS FIRMLY IN PLACE   The other is when the organization is content with the current structure, everyone is "in place," and thus no one is jockeying for positions. This happens most often in a family-owned organization and also in companies where those at the top are young, have many years left in their positions, and are not planning to move to other companies.

WHEN YOU MUST HAVE A MENTOR

WHEN YOUR PEERS DO   There are two times when you must have a mentor to survive, and the first is when your peers have mentors and are beginning to leave you behind due to the extra "shoves" they are receiving. At this time it will be clear that you will need a mentor if you want to get ahead.

WHEN YOUR CONTROVERSIAL BOSS DOES   The second is when your obstructionistic boss is firmly lined up and being mentored by his boss, especially when you find (try though you may) that you are not on their team. At this point, you most definitely need a wise mentor to guide you through the company politics which are bound to follow. If you have ever worked for a boss who continued to rise even though he was ineffective and even offensive (as I once did), then you need to take a good look at his mentor. Why is he included in confidential business meetings? The important luncheons? Why does his career continue to climb? The chances are that he is firmly attached to someone important (or to a company hero), and no one is willing to touch him.

I have seen this happen several times, and probably his mentor is no more effective than he is, but in all likelihood is several years from retirement and no one is willing to rock *his* boat. Now, hard as it may seem, and as unfair, men understand all this. Women must comprehend organizational games better and learn how to fight back. In this case, you can leave, try to get a mentor that outranks your boss's, or play the waiting game. If you can hang on and wait for your boss's mentor to retire, then probably no one will pick your boss to mentor, and you can make your move. With his mentor gone, and his reputation known, you will be amazed how easy it will be! And then the sweet smell of success is yours!

CASES

The three cases below are examples of a woman (Sandra) who had two mentors but at different times, of another (Joanne) who successfully had two at the same time, and of a third (Carole) who had one significant mentor and three lesser ones spread throughout her career.

Sandra Puncsak
Marketing Manager
Singer Company

"I have had two mentors at different times in my career. Both have been at pivotal points; one was a specialist in the public arena and the other later helped me jump into the private sector.

"My most recent and also the most significant mentor was Dan Gardner. I met him when I was Deputy Director of the Portland Job Corps Center. Dan was interested in hiring a woman for his marketing team and was referred to us by the Department of Labor.

"When I found out that Dan came specifically to look at me, I was flattered. My first meeting with him was comfortable and informal, and to be honest, there was an immediate rapport and chemistry between us.

"He offered me the position of western regional marketing manager, and commented that there was not another woman out there marketing for the private sector in that particular type of business. I felt it was a unique opportunity to 'blaze some new trails.'

"I was both curious and interested in how I could fit in with my public sector experience and education, a behavioral sciences background. From our earliest discussions, I could tell that we complemented each other. We shared respect and appreciation for what each had accomplished. Dan was very successful in the marketing field, and was known as a person who 'made things happen.' Once the decision was made for me to join Singer, Dan did all the front end work on my behalf. I never had a formal interview with personnel or other key staff. He later told me there had been much discussion within the company regarding his decision not only to hire a woman, but someone who had not come up through the ranks.

"The formal job offer arrived quicker than I had expected, and at the point where Dan needed my commitment, I began to vacillate. It was an unsettling time for me; I had just made some rather significant personal and professional changes and I felt wounded and vulnerable. I began to be uncertain if I could cope with any more.

"Dan then made a trip to Oregon, where I was working, to clear the air. He has good listening skills, and I found that I was able to discuss my intimate feelings with him. We talked about my relocating, my concern of being an outsider in a predominantly male world, and my insecurity about being able to compete in the marketplace and bring in contracts.

"Dan obviously felt that he could take 'risks' in sharing *his* views about my decision with me. He said, 'You can always opt to stay safe in your present position with the Job Corps and keep your cocoon of friends, but what would that prove?' He threw my words back to me, and said: 'You said you wanted to move ahead, have an opportunity to be successful and visible in the corporate world. Now you have that opportunity and you are afraid to take the risk.'

"He also told me: 'You will not fail. I can and will make things happen. As my star rises, so does yours, and as your star rises, so does mine. You can become the best marketing person in this field. Once you have demonstrated your power and know how to use it, you can go anywhere. I want to help you accomplish your goals.'

"In the early stages of the job, I looked to Dan for nurturing and protection. I needed his help in gaining confidence and poise, in identifying obstacles and navigating through office politics. But when Dan sensed that I relied on him too much, he would step aside and say: 'You are on your own. Take over. You don't need me to do it for you.' Thus, while he was always there to provide constructive criticism and to guide me, he was determined that I take responsibility for my own fate and progress.

"I made it clear that I wanted the opportunity to be 'groomed.' I believe the 'grooming' process in a mentor relationship is not often discussed, and that it is a very important ingredient. It is certainly known that male protegés reflect the standards of their male mentors in such ways as their demeanor, dress, and club memberships. But how does a male mentor discuss some of these items with a female protegée? We had some very interesting conversations in this regard.

"Dan's biggest contribution to my career was in letting me know how others perceived me. It was important to me to come across as competent, astute, and professional. We developed signals which he used if I were talking too fast, using my hands too often, fidgeting, or appearing to be overly friendly or emotional. We talked about posture, style, voice pitch, and my habit of sometimes giving an answer before I had time to digest the question. He said that regardless of my enthusiasm, in the corporate world, this is not a plus. We also talked about healthy manipulation and how to massage people more effectively in order to come out ahead in contract negotiations.

"Because of the demand for extensive travel, close communication, and participation in political, business, and social functions, we worked hard not to be viewed as being so connected as to give rise to suspicion regarding our relationship, mentoring or otherwise. Neither one of us wanted even the suggestion of a physical affair; the relationship was to be one of 'business.' But I have always felt a mentor-protegée arrangement is one of shared intimacy; albeit, not a physical intimacy, but rather one in which ideas, feelings, dreams, frustrations—all the raw emotions—are exposed, discussed, and resolved.

"And I think there is more risk in a male-female relationship than one would find in a similar male-male arrangement and, because of the risk, more intensity and introspection on the part of both parties. The lines of human sexuality and sexual signatures are always drawn and, at some point in the relationship, will have to be confronted.

"There continues to be a bond between Dan and myself—a deep affection and respect for one another. The process of mentoring goes on, but on a different level now. I have learned that we expect so much from our mentors, and then we don't need them anymore. We say, 'That is enough, you are always criticizing me.' I feel I have achieved many of the initial goals I set for myself, redefined others, and established new ones. I would like to think that the relationship has been mutually beneficial, that I contributed and I received. I have appreciated the intellectual and emotional honesty between us and, as a result, I sense a healthiness and strength in having shared this experience.

"Dan's patience, support, and guidance helped to provide an environment of respect and encouragement in which I grew as a secure and confident individual. I enjoyed his telling me: 'You really listen to me and follow through when I make suggestions. There isn't anything more I can teach you,' and 'I would let you handle our business situation on your own. I trust your judgment and observations.'

"I had another significant mentor relationship before I met Dan, when I was a student coordinator in a private, nonprofit corporation, set up by the National Institution of Education. His name was Jake Carlson. In this job I recruited all the students in this program to test out an alternative high school program. My position put me in close proximity with the director. I felt Jake was one of the most intelligent and articulate sources of power and control I'd ever met. It was obvious to me that these qualities were the right ones in order to be successful and to get ahead. It was extremely important to me to emulate these qualities and behavior, and to be closely associated with him. He was a good problem solver and had a special ability to bring together human resources. However, it was Jake who taught me that a mentor relationship, once healthy and positive, can suddenly become nasty and destructive.

"Our staff was small, and in these earlier years we had many hats to wear, which forged a strong bond among the members. We had great loyalty to the concept of the program and to one another.

"To be quite honest, I chose Jake to be my mentor, more than he picked me to play this role. As a result, many of the painful things that came about were because I had such a high esteem and respect for him. I felt that when he later changed, I could no longer hold him in the same light. It was very unsettling for me to see someone change so drastically, and I felt that I could no longer have such high regard for either him or his value systems.

"I know that this sounds crazy, but when Jake became forty, the physical change in him was such a dramatic departure from what we had experienced previously, that the entire structure and health of the organization was threatened and could no longer be sustained under his leadership. The man who usually wore the corporate uniform, the man who always provided guidance and direction, now turned to leisure suits, loafers, and turtle necks.

"By this time, he had formed a close alliance with two of the female staff members; these three formed such a close pack that the rest of us felt anger, resentment, and frustration from being excluded. He guided them, was interested in them, and even socialized with them. He had previously been the type of manager who kept an emotional distance from his staff and was not interested in playing favorites. Formerly, his fair play had kept things in perspective and balance. The small staff was shocked, and the organization began to collapse.

"Even during this time, I still liked Jake. A good relationship continued to be possible as long as I did what he wanted. As he saw me grow, I think he felt proud and pleased with my competence. I felt he took a great deal of the credit for my behavior and abilities.

"I often felt that I ended up giving into him too often, even if I did not agree. I thought he must know more than I did, and thus be right. But soon I gave in too many times, and this made me bitter and angry. To be quite blunt, I suspect now that our mentor relationship reflected some aspects of a parent/child one. As long as I listened and abided by the rules, it went well and doors were opened; when I was naughty or asserted too much independence, I was punished and reprimanded and made to feel I performed less than satisfactorily. Jake would dish out stinging criticism and, especially where I felt successful, he would make me feel there were serious limitations on my part.

"Finally, Jake made the decision to leave and open his own consulting firm. The staff quickly divided into camps. Many felt I was the only one who could run the program; one of Jake's triumvirate announced that she was also interested in being the director. While she had little staff support, she had Jake's blessing, which was of course significant.

"I no longer felt I wanted to be associated with Jake. We had a real conflict over values and goals; he seemed to be going in one direction, and the staff and I in another. It is hard to make the break when you have worked so closely with someone you had held in such high regard. It was gut wrenching!

"The staff wanted things to change and looked for me to confront Jake and seek a more positive direction. I used all my political skills to become the director, and eventually was selected. I found I rejected everything Jake stood for; I even suggested he leave earlier than planned so that the staff could get back to the business of business and re-create their emotional health. It was a very stressful and painful time.

"After I assumed the director's position, it took me a while to bring coherence back into the staff. We worked hard, we talked about what had happened, and agreed that we did not want it to continue. It can be hard for a staff member to assume the leadership role. Where I had participated, I now directed. Role expectations and relationships changed.

"My experience with Jake made me grow and, more importantly, made me understand better both the role of management and the role of office politics in dealing with staff and with expected production. This relationship has made me a better manager in that I now listen and observe more, and notice what is occurring both externally as well as internally.

"I had always felt that Jake added a great deal to my professional life, but I wished I hadn't had to go through some of the nasty experiences that occurred in the organization. After he left, it took almost two years before we could talk closely again, and I could feel comfortable with him. I have since thanked Jake for his influence, and one of our last conversations was in reference to this book. I was able to tell him again that he was one of the most powerful influences in my career, but I have not been able to talk about the events that occurred in the breaking of our relationship. I don't ever want to open up this wound again, and to this day I'm not quite sure how or why it happened.

"I had experienced such a negative reaction to Jake's changes, yet found it hard to let the relationship go. This letting go can be painful, especially when the relationship was such a positive and successful one. When it changes, and your mentor withdraws, it is like saying good-bye, and many of us have a hard time saying good-bye. I learned from our relationship, and I thank him for that. Also, I learned to go on. I was able to deal with conflict, make the program successful, and move ahead in a very positive way.

"Having two mentor experiences made me realize the importance of *being* a mentor, and the role that that person plays in the life of another individual. But even more significant is the responsibility one has for that mentoring process. I ask my mentorees what they want to accomplish and what their expectations are, and what I can do to help them achieve more success. I try to suggest options or alternatives that they may not have thought about themselves. I also tell them to be ready for 'luck' which may be nothing more than opportunity and preparation coming together at the same time.

"A mentor relationship is a very special, intimate one, and people can become very, very close. Without the sexual relationship, people may become even closer because then they take the time to understand moods, anxiety, and frustration.

"As Dan once said, 'Being a mentor is damn hard work.'"

Joanne C. Brem
Senior Marketing Representative
Honeywell Information Systems

"When I came out of college, my first job was with Burroughs Corporation in 1975. My mentor was my zone manager, Gerald Willis, and for the next three years he had a large impact on my professional development. Gerald had been with Burroughs about ten years and we liked each other instantly. We had many conversations over beers, and I let him know I was interested in getting his feedback on how I was doing—he cared about me. The age difference was nine years, and I reported directly to him. I was a most enthusiastic person, and he was very responsible in helping me tone down and act more businesslike.

"Gerald would say: 'Relax, we can make team sales. I am not trying to take the stage from you.' He taught me how to plan calls and make effective presentations. He said: 'Your enthusiasm is so positive, but tone a little of that down.' I learned how to strategize and plan—it is important to have a plan in your career. Another important thing I learned from him was about winning and losing and playing the game. I discovered how many 'tapes I had playing in me that kept me from being successful.' He said: 'What matters is that you win. No one will look at how you played the game if you don't win. If you don't go to win, don't go. Go for the reward of winning.'"

"In September of 1978, Gerald and I were having a conversation about goals when something sparked inside me. I realized I could have either a job or a career. At that moment I made the psychological change and became 'career-oriented.' That desire manifested itself in a new confidence in my abilities. I became smoother at presentations and felt good about it because I was working toward something.

"During this three-year period, I also learned time management from Gerald.He once helped me by saying, 'You need to be more organized!' We would discuss prioritizing at the Phoenix Monday morning staff meetings — that is still my weak point professionally.

"Part of my development was a decision to move to the Bay Area. I asked Gerald for his advice on telling our branch manager. He recommended approaches on doing this, and said to 'go for it' if that was what I wanted. He said, 'You can do whatever you want to do.' I remember how scared I was. He said, 'Let people know what you want and believe you can do.' He did not write a recommendation or help—I did this on my own. I went to the San Jose Burroughs office and met a woman whom I thought I wanted to work for. Gerald did talk to me about negotiations and for example, told me to make sure they paid for half of the moving expenses—I would not have done this. I made the move in February of 1979. I went into a new environment which allowed me to make the changes I wanted to implement.

"Now Gerald and I are good friends. I saw him recently and we brought each other up to date on our careers. He said, 'I can't believe how you've changed and how your confidence has gone up.'

"I have had other mentors also. Through college and my first year with Burroughs, I had a good relationship with a man nine years older than I was, Sterling Watts. He was getting his M.B.A., and I was going to be a probation officer. I grew up in a background which included many niceties, travel, and entertainment, and he asked me how I was going to support myself in this manner. He got me interested in taking business courses. Next, Sterling helped me when I went out on interviews. He sat me down, boosted my confidence, and helped me write my letters, resume, and plan my trip to interview in San Francisco. He encouraged me to go into business, and when I did, Sterling provided personal support during my first year of adjusting to the work world.

"At the same time that I knew Gerald, I knew another man who was also successful at Burroughs, and who also acted as a lesser mentor. It was interesting to have two mentors at the same time, and I did not feel a conflict having this relationship with both men. He was a very powerful person, and I found his input invaluable in my growing perceptions of the 'big picture' of business. We had good rapport, and he once told me I should be more at ease and to talk about business after work—that I had lots to learn and could learn it after work over drinks. He used to quiz me and test me on what my responses would be in different sales situations. I would say, 'I don't want to talk about business,' and he would say, 'Come on, be a little more astute and spontaneous.' He has just been promoted and is doing incredibly well.

"A few years passed since we last saw each other. He called recently and after we talked, said, 'I just can't believe this woman I am hearing —you just exude confidence.' Now we are reestablishing somewhat of a mentor relationship. We talked several times on the telephone recently, and he advised me. I can sense that he will be a big help at Honeywell. He said, 'Go for the heart, be sharp politically—this is the most important thing.'

"Four months ago, I wanted a particular account management position with Honeywell, which I did not get. He said, 'What did you do about it?' I replied, 'I talked to my branch marketing manager and also with several peers about it.' We talked for over an hour about going for what you want in a company, and about going over people's heads. He is good at corporate politics, and I can learn a lot from him. He told me to watch who is in power at our meetings. Our western regional manager is one such person at Honeywell. Two months back, this man told me: 'It is very important to have a sponsor at this company if you want to go anywhere.' I should have asked, 'What can I do about it?'

While I do not see him becoming a mentor, I know he believes in me. He once asked me, 'When are you going to be a millionaire?' He is the first person who ever suggested I could be a millionaire. Maybe I can do this—it's a new goal I have; it is nice to have someone think I can do it. He has great confidence in my power and ability. Through this relationship, I have learned that there is a definite distinction between someone who offers you advice and an occasional talk, and a mentor, who really cares about where you are going and who will support you to make sure it is in the right direction.

"We need to break through barriers and learn how far we can go; we need to lay our cards on the table, but we need people to tell us what the cards are and which ones to play. I talked to my new mentor about this conversation, and he told me to call my regional manager and follow up on his remarks to me about the importance of sponsors. Another thing he told me was to inform this man that I want an account management position. My reply was, 'The one I want is taken,' but he said, 'Joanne, tell him now and why you would be good at it. This will line you up for another account manager position when one comes open.' I am learning that it is valuable to know what to say to whom and when.

"Subsequently I met with my regional manager and discussed my future with Honeywell and what I want, as well as his remarks about sponsors. He said that the way it really works is 'I pat your back, you pat mine.' This is absolutely true in business!

"Even up to two years ago, I didn't know what a mentor was. Along with realizing the importance of time in your life, you need to realize that there are select people who can help you, depending upon your area of concern. You have to be able to identify the things that you need help with and who specifically can help you with them. You don't talk with these people unless they understand. They need to understand the situation if they are to help you. I realized that there are not that many people who can help me and have learned to really qualify the people I talk to.

"I believe that I have also helped my mentors' careers. I have been told that I am one of their most valuable inputs, and one of the first corporated women who is successful in the computer industry, formerly a world of men. They have asked me for input on women, especially in interviewing, because they felt I could tell if other women could be successful in sales. Men have told me they liked my approach, that many women do not work well with men's value systems, and that they appreciated my honesty.

"In the past year, I have become increasingly conscious of how much I am using my mentors' knowledge all the time to benefit myself. I find that nobody objects to spending some of their time with me, if my line of questioning is well thought out and presented intelligently. Once a mentor knows that you are indeed a competent person who is 'going somewhere,' he will take a really active interest and concern in your welfare. This can make the difference."

Carole Westphal
Staff Director
Business Product Manager
Pacific Telephone & Telegraph

"I have been staff director, business product management, for about one year, but I have been with the Bell System for about twelve years.

"Mentors have played an important role in my own career. I have had one significant mentor and three less significant ones, who have helped me get where I am today. They helped me with my own mental image and with my perception of what I was capable of doing in the business. They also paved the way for me in fields where women have just about never been. I am the only woman at my level in marketing at Pacific Telephone. It takes more than just hard work to get ahead. This is where mentors have been helpful—by getting people to recognize my hard work where it was important.

"My first mentor was Geoff Scott, who is a division level manager in engineering in Sacramento—the level at which I am now. I met Geoff by working in his division; he took over when the previous manager retired. My first impression of him was one of sheer terror. He is about six feet five inches tall and a red-headed Scot, also one of the loudest men I have ever met. He had an automatic door closer on his door, and when you would sit down, he would close the door from his desk. He scared the living daylights out of me.

"I decided I was not going to be intimidated by Geoff. The turning point came one day when I was leaving at 6 p.m. I said, 'I am just making up for coming in late.' He laughed, and from then on the relationship became far more personal in terms of his counseling me on the direction I should take in the company. It really is because of him that I switched into the marketing department and moved to San Francisco. There are not as many career opportunities in Sacramento, but because I had a lot of credibility in my department, I was reluctant to leave and start fresh.

"First of all, Geoff made the initial contact, set up the interview, and did some advance PR, so it was really easy to make the transition. He gave me the 'kick in the pants' to get out and move. He took a risk to recommend me, and had faith in my work.

"I still keep in touch with him. He is one of the first people I call when I get a raise or a promotion. However, we don't have a mentor relationship anymore. I am on his level, and he will retire in a few years.

"When I came to San Francisco, I met Jim Miller, an assistant vice president and now my boss. He came into the department as department head the same day that I came in as product manager, so we were both brand new. I didn't really get to know him until about a year later when I began working in an area of high visibility in the company, the Centrex product. This is the telephone switching system that many big companies in San Francisco are using. Another executive was managing another product as well as Centrex. They decided it was too much for one person and gave me Centrex. I got it because they felt the other product was more important! My philosophy was the same as in all the other jobs I have had. I took the job and levered it a level higher than when I came in. Jim helped me to do this. I started to make enough noise so that people would recognize what I could do, and he helped me to do this.

"I am now a level four in management. The president is at level eight, so I am in the middle. When I came to work for Jim, I was at the second level. He promoted me to the third level. He advised strongly that I needed field management experience. He then negotiated the job for me; it is almost impossible to go from staff with no previous field experience to third level in the field. I went to Oakland and managed the real estate marketplace for Northern California. All telecommunication sales to real estate or title companies were my responsibility for one year. Jim was my 'shoe horn out.' I was frightened, and I wondered what many of the people thought of me, a young woman with no experience coming in to be their manager.

"It was an exciting year for me because we had the best sales results in the country. That was the first time I realized that people like to work for me. I had not had a large staff before. People gladly worked for me and had a good time at it. I also found that my basic management style is that of 'player-coach.' I am not very good at delegating and letting go. I like to get involved and be a part of the team. I become the leader only when they need a leader. This was something I learned about myself. Jim helped me understand some of these things.

"After I got myself underwritten as a line manager, Jim promoted me one year later to a fourth level manager. I loved the field, but chose not to pass up the promotion because it was a rare one. There were three of us at first, but one retired, and now two of us are doing what three used to do. I asked for and got the bulk of the assignment, and it almost finished me.

"At the same time, I tried to go to school and start an M.B.A. program. I felt free enough to tell Jim I wasn't meeting my commitments, and he said, 'Don't worry about it.' He promised to let me know if there was a serious problem. He helped me with delegating work—this has to be the hardest skill to learn. If you are competent, it is hard to let things go. He said, 'You can send this here and this there.' Probably teaching me to delegate responsibility was the biggest thing he has done for me this year.

"Next fall I am going to be a Sloan Fellow at the Stanford Graduate School of Business for one academic year. I dropped the M.B.A. program when the offer to get an M.S. from Stanford was made, and I am looking forward to the opportunity to expand my contacts and knowledge beyond my present corporate experience.

"Currently, I am acting as a mentor to two other women. I think one of them, Sally, is still a little startled that I have selected her to mentor. She is like a sponge and learns everything I teach her. She is willing to work hard and take chances because she knows that high rewards are nearly always accompanied by commensurate risks. She started as a clerk for the company, and within two years I promoted her to second level management. I then found her a line management position so she can earn her stripes. I got someone to take my word that she is an 'untested but very capable woman' and give her a chance in the field. She is identified on a special middle management program, and I have no reservations that she will do well. She told me she was truly gratified that I selected her to counsel and help.

"My relationship with the other woman, Louise, is one of being a personal friend as well as a mentor. I sponsored her, and she is now also at second level management. We spend a lot of time talking about her career and in which direction she should be moving. She, too, has a lot of potential and all of the outstanding qualities that Sally has.

"I consider myself fortunate in having had the support and guidance of several very helpful mentors. Thus, I feel it is now my turn to give special coaching and aid to promising younger women coming along."

CHAPTER FIVE

Sex and the Mentor Relationship

Probably the biggest thing that Kirsten's mentor did was to encourage her to run for Congress. He later acted as her campaign manager and, according to her, the relationship was also very difficult, as normally candidates don't live with their managers.

Linda's mentor was instrumental in bridging her educational gap so that she could become a competent career person. Later, the mentor relationship ended along with the termination of their personal one.

DOES SEXUAL INVOLVEMENT HELP IN THIS JOB?

Sex is a topic that does need to be addressed when discussing the entire mentor relationship. Because of the close nature of the mentor function, the relationship is a close, caring one; there is time spent together discussing meaningful problems and situations. There is a turning to each other to share victories as well as defeats. As pointed out earlier, the mentor feeling can be one of intense devotion. If you like and admire your mentor, how can you work closely with him *without* loving him?

70

It would appear that out of all mentor relationships, maybe even as high as one-fifth (as documented by my research) involve some kind of sexual contact. When a man first offers close sponsorship to a woman, she has to wonder what he expects in return. At some deep level, body chemistry, with all the complexities of sex, enters in and must be defined. Boundaries need to be made clear so that both parties are comfortable.

As Viewed by Peers, Subordinates, Supervisors   Sex with one's mentor is very complex, and the full ramifications are still not fully understood. What is understood is it can almost destroy either party's credibility. A definite breakdown of communication can follow with one's peers as well as with subordinates. The result can be a very disruptive and dysfunctional experience for superiors as well. Not only can the mentoree be resented, but she can experience feelings of open hostility. She will be perceived as "privileged," the recipient of special favors and information, and because of this, others will feel insecure, threatened, and even unfairly treated.

Co-workers' feelings of frustration, even though not always necessary, will lead them to feel that they cannot get ahead no matter how hard they work or how well they perform. Any advancement to the mentoree's career will be seen as a result of sexual favors only, and not due to her ability. As long as sexual involvement is openly occurring, an atmosphere of bitterness, gossip, and hostility will continue to grow.

A Negative Affair   A well-known example of how sex does *not* help on the job is the Mary Cunningham/William Agee affair at Bendix. Whether or not they had a sexual affair became secondary; what was crucial is that the employees at Bendix *perceived* their relationship this way. Agee, chairman of the Bendix Corporation, hired Cunningham as his executive assistant, promoted her to vice president for corporate and government affairs a year later, and two months after that, promoted her again to vice president for strategic planning. This made Cunningham, at age 29, one of the highest-ranking young women in American industry—for all of two weeks.

This is a classic example of the effect that a true mentor can have on the upward mobility of his mentoree's career. The unfortunate results of the Cunningham example are well known: Agee called a meeting of over 600 Bendix employees to announce that he and Cunningham were "close friends" but that that had nothing to do with her promotions. The drama lies in the fact that Cunningham's effectiveness was never questioned. Not only did she have a coveted Harvard M.B.A. to her credit, but she had a superior track record at Bendix as well.

As a result, Cunningham lost her effectiveness to operate, her resignation from Bendix was soon accepted by the board, and Agee's credibility and judgment were seriously questioned. At one point, the rumors and stories about his personal behavior and romantic involvement with Cunningham even threatened to end his tenure as the head of the company. A prominent Bendix board member, Robert W. Purcell, resigned, stating that he had "lost confidence in the company's top management." While he did not state specifically why, it was attributed to Agee's handling of the embarrassing rumors about his relationship with Cunningham.

WILL SEX BRING THE NEXT BIG PROMOTION?

MORE HARM THAN GOOD   While a sexual involvement may increase the intimacy of the relationship for the moment, the evidence shows that it seems to do more harm than good in the long run. In fulfilling his sexual needs, a mentor may put himself and his desires ahead of you and your career. He can, without your knowledge, not recommend you for the next big promotion or geographical move. He can keep your apprenticeship and dependence on him far longer than is in your best interest.

THE DOUBLE STANDARD AT WORK   Unfortunately, there is still the "double standard" at work. A sexual encounter by a man does not have the negative effect on his career that it can have on a woman's. And still more unfortunate, sexual activity can make the woman appear less dedicated to her work, not to be taken seriously, and results in general loss of power and credibility.

There is a lot of speculative judging by the organization, and thus one does need to pay attention to appearances. Travel together, attendance at nonbusiness functions, leaving late at night or arriving together early in the morning can give an appearance that can be counterproductive to one's co-workers. It is important for the mentor and the mentoree to foster understanding among their colleagues as to the nature of the mentor-mentoree relationship. Peers especially need to know that it is not based on sex. There is no evidence to suggest sex with one's mentor *ever* qualified, or in any way assisted, one in achieving their next big promotion.

A recent article in the *Wall Street Journal* made two interesting comments. First, it stated: "Despite all the talk of women 'sleeping their way up' in an organization, most of the women interviewed could not think of a single instance. One woman, who was divorced and thirty when she became the organization's first female vice president, says, 'If all the rumors about my sleeping my way up were true, I wouldn't be able to walk!!'"

The paper's second interesting comment was made by Barbara Sayre Casey, then a vice president of Kaufman and Broad, Inc., a Los Angeles home builder, in response to a man who once asked whom she slept with to get her job. "I was so offended," she recalled. "I am sure others thought it, but he was the only one crude enough to ask. I told him, 'The chairman, the president, and all the members of the board!'"

REASONS FOR
THE UNIFORM ANSWER: DON'T!

Professional women who have experienced some form of sexual contact appear to be unified in their advice to younger women coming up the corporate ladder. In a word: DON'T! It's not worth it in the long run.

THE WOMAN STILL LOSES   In fact, this was the only question on the survey answered by over 400 professional women in which there was *total* agreement. Of those responding, 100 percent answered "no" to the question: "If you have had sex with your mentor (which one-fifth replied they had), do you advise it?" I thought it especially meaningful that the one-fifth who had had sex with their mentors uniformly said, "Don't do it!"

In a sexual situation, respondees pointed out, it is almost always the woman's reputation that suffers. Often when the affair ends, it is the woman who gets transferred or fired; the mentor, being higher, is the one to stay. Thus, there is still the double standard. Women quite often are more emotional over the breakup, and this can cause their work to suffer. She can also feel that she has "lost face."

A MORAL ISSUE   For most professional people, sex is still a moral issue. Most professional people in our society do equate morality with sexuality, and to see a colleague lax in his morals or judgment in one area often means he is lax in other areas as well. It is wholly unacceptable if either party entering a sexual relationship is married. The man, no matter how senior, is made to look foolish; the woman manipulative and cunning.

Cynthia Fuchs Epstein, professor of sociology at Queens College and co-director of the Center for Social Sciences at Columbia University, states that "sexual relationships with mentors are not inevitable, but frequent." She says, "This can work to a woman's advantage or disadvantage. The advantage is that if a woman's mentor or sponsor is accomplished and knowledgeable, she'll learn a lot more from him because of the time they spend together outside of work. On the other hand, people are apt to attribute the woman's ideas and work to the man, and to resent her. Typically it's the woman's reputation that suffers. People rarely say, 'Oh, hasn't *he* improved as a result of their affair.' And of course, if the sexual relationship ends, she's the subordinate and the old 'last-hired, first-fired' rule may apply."

If the relationship becomes a serious one, and the mentor should marry his mentoree, then I feel the mentor relationship is bound to change over time. Certainly, the relationship will become more equal. I do not think one can continue to mentor the person who becomes his spouse. If you are close and more or less equal in one relationship, it is difficult to be professional and maintain a superior/subordinate one in another. Thus, in time, the nature of the relationship is bound to alter. In fact, some women might have climbed even higher if they had *not* married their mentors!

When discussing this part of my book, one of my mentors, with a twinkle in his eye, sent me the following: "It occurs to me that one should not duck the item of sex and the mentor, which might reasonably be of interest to any young woman pondering the possible advantages and the possible hazards of forming a mentor/protegée relationship with a man, however distinguished, wise, or attractive. The impressive adverse response to your questionnaire permits at least two possible interpretations, i.e., moral objections or practical considerations. For the purpose of this discussion, we can and should leave the moral issues to the individual. The practical considerations deserve our attention.

"First, it should be understood that nothing in the mentor concept implies any obligation to become involved in a social, extracurricular relationship outside the context of the normal business relationship.

"Further, when both parties are in the employ of the same organization, the development of an emotional (or sexual) attachment will tend to distort and destroy the validity and usefulness of the relationship to the institution. Even legitimate favors or opportunities arranged for the protegée will be suspect as favoritism, and she may reasonably wonder whether her career is to depend, not on her competence, but on her sexual performance.

"Finally, it should be noted that this problem does not arise often, despite the lurid attention it gets in paperback novels and sometimes in the media. And a woman of some tact and sophistication can avoid it without seriously offending a too eager admirer. Amen."

CASES

These two examples are different: Kirsten's close relationship with her mentor turned out favorably (and contradicts the belief that one cannot maintain a mentor relationship if married), and Linda's, in the long run, did not.

Kirsten Olsen
Investment Broker
Smith Barney Harris Upham & Company, Inc.

"I have been with Smith Barney for less than one year; before this I was with Paine Webber for four years, and before that, with Merrill Lynch for three years. I met my first mentor, Jim Dolan, in 1967 while I was head of operations for Dean Witter, and he was a client of the office. Jim became my mentor when I went to work for him and helped him start an electronics company in 1968 called Drexler Technology.

"Jim is a very interesting and dynamic person, and he asked me for advice when he was thinking about starting his own company. I became the assistant to the president (Jim), and, when we went public, I became head of public relations. I looked at acquisitions and new products. The company did great at first, then poorly in the last recession, but it is now doing well again.

"Jim, who is about twenty years older than I am, essentially gave me the college degree that I needed in business. I could not have gotten ahead without this knowledge. Although he is no longer a mentor, he is still a friend and advisor. I had only taken a few busines courses in the evening at a local college, and he taught me enough to give the equivalent of an M.B.A. degree. During the time we worked together, we worked eighty hours a week and would then be on the telephone in the evening. I also worked every Saturday for five years. It was a very close, beneficial relationship; there was a lot of trust, and we confided things to each other about all aspects of our lives.

"I helped Jim professionally by being a sounding board. I have good common sense, which was very important to him. Jim would come up with ideas—he is a real genius in business—and we would discuss them. Thus I felt our relationship was very worthwhile for him as well.

"I worked for Jim for five years, and now we are friends, but not as close. In fact, it was only in the last year that we have renewed our relationship and become friends again. In 1978, Jim put me down when I ran for Congress, and I told him I didn't want to see him or talk to him. He said afterwards that it was a great idea that I ran, but he certainly didn't encourage me at the time. I honestly think he was jealous! Running for Congress gave me great self-confidence, and it was also good for business. I now feel I can approach anyone. I have run twice (I am a Democrat), and I was much better the last time. At the moment, I don't have any political ambitions, and instead plan to work at my career as an investment broker. And currently I am discovering that I have a real interest in wealth and power!

"I have recently begun to see Jim more frequently because our brokerage firm has recommended his stock. It is a funny feeling. Now our relationship is more of an equal one, and he is quite complimentary to me. I am glad that our relationship is more stable.

"I have had two other mentors. The first, Eric Brown, is a venture capitalist. I met him at an annual meeting of Intersil at the Bankers Club. I have met some wonderful people there, including the man who is now my husband. Eric is a magnetic personality, a Renaissance man. He also consoled me when I was going through some personal problems in 1975. He helped me with lots of business ideas and encouraged me to be a broker. I am still friends with him, but the mentor relationship has ended.

"Eric liked my common sense approach. There is a fifteen-year age difference between us, and he enjoyed being my mentor and helping me. He is still my client, and we talk probably at least once a week. We are not as close, but we have lunch a few times a year. The relationship ended when I improved and did not need his help as much. I had absorbed what he had to offer. Also, I changed mentors—my husband became my mentor—and when that relationship got going, the other one ended. It is hard to have more than one relationship of this kind at the same time.

"My next mentor, Tim Sherman, is now my husband. He is vice president and general counsel for Advanced Micro Devices. Tim was running for Congress at the time I met him but did not make it through the primaries. He had his own law firm at the time, and I worked briefly in his campaign and stole his mailing lists! He became my mentor when I met him again a year later, and he introduced me to a lot of people who soon after became my clients. He also gave me great advice about developing business in sales and in meeting people. Tim is eight years older than I am, and I feel he has brought me to a higher level of being. He is one of the most intelligent people I have ever known, and he continues to spur me on.

"We have been married for five years and Tim is still my mentor. He likes our relationship, and we bounce ideas off each other. It is a good and sound partnership. I am able to give him a sounding board of ideas for both his company and his career. I encourage him to meet people who I feel are the right people to meet. I also make him more disciplined than he would be otherwise. And he spurs me on by saying, 'Why don't you do this?' It is a close intellectual and caring relationship.

"Probably the biggest thing Tim did was to encourage me to run for Congress in both 1978 and in 1980. This was the biggest thing I ever did—an all-out effort. He first mentioned it when we were discussing our goals for the year, and I mentioned that I'd like to work in a campaign. He said, 'Why don't you run?' and I said, 'For what?' and he suggested Congress. He then went to New York for one week on business, and when he returned, he said, 'Are you ready?' and I replied, 'Why not! What do I have to lose except my health and my sanity?' He was my campaign manager, and he helped me with both my strategy and my speeches. As a lawyer, he is very articulate. He used to be a journalist as well as a political science teacher, so his views were very savvy and helpful.

"However, it was also very difficult, as normally candidates don't live with their campaign managers. When we would be going to bed, Tim would say, 'Oh, we forgot to do this.' We could never relax! He has an extremely high level of energy. The first time I ran, I received 58 percent of the vote in the primary; the last time I got 62 percent. I ran against one opponent in each primary. The first time I spent $60,000; the last time, $5,000. Visibility made this difference. I financed the campaigns by starting with my clients, who were very supportive. The labor unions helped me because they wanted out the incumbent, a Republican, who was against the maritime unions. I raised money essentially by going to people who opposed this man. I am the only woman who ever won a primary in this district, which I thought was great.

"During the campaigns, Tim helped bring me back down to earth. It was very heady being the candidate. Others pep you up and flatter you, and it is very hard to be realistic. He made me focus on the real world. At the end of the campaign, I reacted badly. It is one thing to lose, but it is another thing to read about it. It took me a couple of months to recuperate. I got better press the first time; the last time they didn't like me because they thought I was too conservative. Also, I had recently had a baby. I thought this might get special press as a human interest story; but instead, it was used in a negative way.

"Last year I made $48,000. This year I should make between $60,000 and $100,000. I like money because there is a certain power and status in knowing you can do it yourself. I have some separate property, and it is very important for me to have my own base. Every woman should feel good about her finances, both current and future.

"The great thing about moving ahead in one's career is that I am now a mentor not only to young women, but young men also. It is gratifying being on the mentor side—a very satisfying experience that I hope to continue."

Linda Farmer
Manager, Office of Field Education
Amdahl Corporation

"My mentor was Charles Arders, systems programmer and member of the technical staff at ESL. We met at ESL, although we were in different departments. I had a nontechnical job, and Charlie's organization used the services of my department. He would come by and talk to me and, at this time I was a key punch operator. I had graduated from high school and was taking some evening courses at a local junior college. I was just getting involved in data processing; Charlie saw me as someone with both interest and commitment.

"I was spending my lunch hour doing homework for my classes. Charlie saw that the classes I took were related to his profession, and he was very helpful. Our relationship started with his general assistance in discussing the exercises at the beginning of my textbook chapters. I felt a lot of admiration and respect for him.

"We were both married at the time, so there was no personal relationship involved. He was very useful to me, as were several other members of the technical staff. They encouraged me to continue my classes and arranged a transfer for me into the technical services department in computer operations. While I worked here, the department continued to support my interests, to the extent of giving me time off during the day to take further classes.

"At a certain point, my marriage started to break up, and my husband and I decided to live apart. I gave some thought to going back to school full-time because I had taken all the courses in my field given at the junior college. I had been promoted into applications programming, and I could see that within ESL if I wanted to advance, I could not do so without a college degree. I had been an English major in high school, and I did not have the math background that I felt I needed. So I was at a juncture where I needed to decide if I was going for a serious career.

"My mentor was very influential and encouraged me to apply to Berkeley instead of a local college (he was a Berkeley graduate). My exposure to academia had been so slight that I did not realize the significance at the time of having a degree from one of the most prestigious colleges in the computer field. So, I applied to Berkeley under Charlie's guidance and completed my degree in computer science a few years later. I continued to work for ESL during the summer; they were very supportive and even paid my tuition at Berkeley.

"Thus Charlie encouraged me all along, suggested Berkeley, counseled me to attend, and made substantial contributions in both moving me into an engineering career and in certain other key decisions. We discussed long-range goals: What would I be doing in five or ten years? I had some clear-cut objectives as to what I wanted to do; I knew also what I did *not* want to do, but I did not know how to avoid these pitfalls. I knew I did not want a lot of late night work or on-call hours as the person responsible when the machines are down. Although it turned out that I did later take a job that had substantial responsibilities in this area, at that time I was ready for it.

"The most important things that Charlie did for me were twofold: First, he helped me bridge the gap between the nonprofessional and the professional; and second, he helped me understand that this was possible.

"Just before I went to Berkeley, Charlie and I were beginning to develop a personal relationship. After my graduation from Berkeley, I returned to ESL and moved in with Charlie full-time. By then, Charlie had changed companies, but he continued to give me career counsel. He was six years ahead of me professionally; he graduated in 1969, and I graduated in 1975. He is actually several years younger than I chronologically. What I discovered when I returned to ESL was that it is very difficult for people to recast you as a professional in spite of your new skills if you have been a nonprofessional. I felt the managers were still thinking, 'There goes the key punch operator.' It was difficult to receive the same kind of responsibilities as someone who had come in with a college degree and was an unknown. It is probably impossible for human nature to make this change!

"Then I switched companies and moved to Control Data. They had a resume of mine from when I graduated from Berkeley, and they recruited me. I had been talking to IBM also. I became a marketing support analyst for Control Data for their cybernetic division. It was great going in as a professional and being perceived in this new role. This was a real growth period for me, and I really enjoyed working there.

"I was there about thirteen months and then went to work at Amdahl. During my employment at Amdahl, Charlie and I decided to start our own company. The company was an outgrowth of some needs of a company that his brother owned. At first, neither of us quit our employment; but since then, Charlie has been working at this company full time. The mentor relationship got in trouble when somewhere along the line I began to question some of Charlie's judgments. When we began to operate the company, there were a lot of his decisions that I questioned. We also decided to get married. I think that my questioning his calls or judgments caused great distress in our relationship. I know it was very important to him that he always keep the lead, and when that lead narrowed too much, it was very threatening.

"I felt he would think, 'Yes, I am getting good professional ideas, but I don't need them from my *wife*. I need somebody who thinks *I* know.' Working with someone when your finances are tied up with his can be difficult. It is salvageable if you can keep your distance. People have a need to be respected in their professional capacities. If they can't get that at home, for goodness sakes, it's tough! If your wife says, 'That was really a stupid mistake,' and can substantiate it on technical grounds, then that becomes a disaster!

"Some people can handle this with less ego than others, or with more tact. But I think this was a real watershed for Charlie and me. Recently Charlie and I have parted, and I waived all my rights to the company in the process of our divorce. He bought my stock when we separated. Charlie subsequently had a relationship with someone at work who was approximately on the same level as I was when I met him. Over a couple of years, he also took the time to 'grow' this person. I think Charlie has a personal need to be a mentor. It would be nice if he could be supportive on a strictly professional basis.

"After we were married, Charlie continued to act in the mentor role of giving advice and counsel. This lasted during our entire marriage. The mentor relationship terminated only when the personal relationship ended. It has to. Although I have known some relationships to continue professionally, it is highly unlikely that a mentor relationship will continue beyond this point.

"I am now remarried and am expecting our first child. All I can say is that it is important to take advantage of unique opportunities as they occur in your career, and, if you are fortunate enough to have a mentor, to capitalize on the many positive aspects of the relationship for as long as they are there."

CHAPTER SIX

When the Relationship Ends

Then he died. They found out that he had cancer in April, and he lasted five more months. Penny later said that it was a relationship she would never replace, that no one would ever know her as well during a particular stage of her career.

Anne's mentor couldn't handle it when she left him. The others in her office said he was acting like a rejected suitor. Later, she recalled that their parting was a time of much conflict.

PASSING YOUR MENTOR FOR GREATER HEIGHTS

WHEN IS YOUR APPRENTICESHIP OVER? Many times in careers, women can pass their mentors. This happens more with men, because if women select a mentor who is near the top, fewer women are promoted to this level and thus do not have the opportunity to pass their male mentors. A good mentor has your interests at heart, is proud and feels somewhat responsible when you are selected and promoted to new heights. He will let you "come and go" in the relationship. Moreover, the mature mentor will help you to assess when your apprenticeship should end and when you are at the point in your career that you no longer want or need his guidance.

There always comes a point where the relationship needs to change. When you feel you have "made it," you need this recognition and acknowledgment from your mentor.

GUARDING AGAINST A COMMON SYNDROME: OVERDEPENDENCY ON MEN   Women are culturally trained to be dependent on males from early childhood, and this overdependency is a common syndrome. Women must guard against any impulse not to pass men, especially when they feel almost certain that it is time for the relationship to end.

Mentors can also be outgrown intellectually, even if you are not promoted over them. You may feel clearly that you have learned almost all that you can from them. At this time, the close protegée relationship needs to be terminated and a more distant relationship, with the two almost as colleagues, put in its place. When you cut the mentor relationship, most often the support and loyalty can still continue.

EXPERIENCING YOUR MENTOR AS UNRECEPTIVE AND DESTRUCTIVE   If the protegée relationship is continued too long beyond its usefulness, you may never have the feelings or the courage to "let go." As pointed out earlier, there are many reasons why the positive mentor relationship can suddenly turn negative, and the protegée may need to be reminded that most mentor relationships are cyclical in nature. Although most often the nature of the unreceptive and destructive behavior can be understood or justified, on occasion it is beyond a simple explanation. Prejudice and chauvinism may overpower earlier qualities. Your mentor may have experienced a shift in his career focus or in his place among the hierarchy, and unfortunately some situations result not only in the loss of a mentor but forever of a friend as well.

TRUSTING YOURSELF TO "FLY UP" (WITHOUT GUILT)   There comes a time in one's career when it is necessary to fly alone. If one does not seize the opportunity for the promotion or new duties, it may never come again. How many older women do you know who have been in the identical job for over ten years? It is possible to crush one's initiative as well as one's hunger for upward mobility. When you are ready to end the relationship, you will know it and should trust your intuition to move and/or "fly up" without guilt.

LOSING YOUR MENTOR AND SURVIVING

WHEN IT ENDS   What happens if you suddenly lose your mentor? There are many factors that contribute to the loss of this relationship. He could die, or move away, or you could be transferred. Or, often enough, there could be a serious conflict which permanently damages the relationship. This can happen between the best of friends, in marriages, or between children, and certainly it happens in the best of mentor relationships. Losing a mentor can be almost as emotionally devastating as the loss of a parent, spouse, or other member of the family. There can be the overwhelming knowledge that no one can ever again take that particular person's place in your professional life.

Not only is the mentor relationship a complex one but it can be a cyclical one as well. There can be negative effects as well as positive ones. You can lose emotional ties with your mentor if you perceive him as selfish, narcissistic, too controlling, and even destructive to your career. He may fall into the "I need constant adoring" syndrome. He can also decide he doesn't *want* to be your mentor, that you are no longer useful, and that he would rather be attached to someone younger and newer to the organization. Or in a moment of great career crisis, your mentor can suddenly let you down by showing no interest in the situation or by failing to give needed guidance. If trust goes, it is hard, if not impossible, to keep the relationship. If a mentor says he will assist you in a particular way (i.e., new title, membership on a committee) and doesn't come through, or worse, doesn't discuss why, it is hard to maintain the same level of respect and confidence. Once this happens, most mentor relationships do not recover. Often great stress, rejection, bewilderment and lowered self-esteem may follow and will need to be dealt with.

COMBATTING MAJOR CHANGES IN COMPANY POLITICS   Your mentor may have negative effects on your career if he falls from grace with his higher-ups and no longer has the ability to be influential on your behalf. This can occur if there is a change in the corporate executives at the top, or a change in the company politics. Once this happens, and your mentor topples, major changes often follow in the organizational structure. Your mentor's enemies, once perceived as your allies, may gun for you. You may have a hard time finding a place in the new power group. When your mentor first perceives *he* is in the downhill side of a power struggle, he may, in his growing need to be looked up to, try to tighten the relationship with you still more. Thus you should be aware of all the dangers of what I call the "tightening noose" syndrome.

COPING WHEN YOU CANNOT FIND A MENTOR

Whatever the reasons for the end of your mentor relationship, it should not put an end to the importance of future mentor relationships for you. So how do you cope?

DEALING WITH STRESS   First, you need to acknowledge the loss of a mentoring relationship can be a most stressful and traumatic experience. The longer and more involved the relationship, the greater the severity of loss symptoms. A "separation shock" occurs, almost like a period of mourning, in which the case study respondents reported feeling such symptoms as "waves of depression," "numbness," "lack of interest in food," "anxiety," "insomnia," "nausea," "self-pity," and a general sense of "being cut off from the real world."

However, there is healing in the process of mourning, and you should not suppress these feelings. Mourning is a way for us to vent our inner emotions, and this ventilation is necessary if we are to continue to grow. Its effect is to heal our psychic wounds so we can free ourselves from the past and start the process of living, working, and being open to a new relationship in the future.

CAPITALIZE ON OTHER RELATIONSHIPS   What else should you do when you cannot find a mentor? You can put emphasis and capitalize on other helpful relationships—supportive bosses, influential friends higher in the organization, loyal peers, women's networks, professional support systems, and sustaining friends. Not only will this "collective" group support you and make you feel better, but they can aid you in your career as well.

RENEW YOUR SEARCH FOR AN EVEN HIGHER MENTOR Also, you can renew your search for a new mentor, perhaps with different influences, one who could be helpful in an area where the old mentor wasn't. Maybe aim for a mentor higher up in the organization, even one with national visibility. In doing so, you should employ all the techniques listed earlier in the chapter "Selecting a Mentor."

Gail Sheehy in *Passages* says that even the best mentors must usually be abandoned if the protegée is to reach full maturity. She states: "Sooner or later every apprentice must refute the absolute power of the mentor if he (or she) is to emerge as owner of his own authority."[1] Thus mentor relationships, like all others, will come to an end. Be ready for this and consider in advance how you will cope when it happens to you.

CASES

The following two women experienced different mentor situations. Penny had a mentor who died and left her. Susan chose to end the relationship when it was no longer useful to her.

Penny L. Kerry
President
PNI

"I met my mentor, Rod Miller, when he interviewed and hired me in July 1970. The relationship developed when I worked temporarily for him for six weeks as his secretary. He was the western division managing architect for Bank Building Corporation, a nationwide architectural firm. After six weeks I received a permanent offer from IBM, where I had previously worked. Rod sat me down and asked where I wanted to go, and what I wanted to do. I knew he was interested in having me stay,

[1] Gail Sheehy, *Passages: Predictable Crises in Adult Life* (New York: E. P. Dutton, 1974), p. 157.

and he asked me not to do anything until after the weekend. On Monday, his firm offered me the administrative assistant position to the division manager, and I said yes. I thought that architecture would be a very glamorous business.

"When I went to work for the division manager, I found out he was an incredible chauvinist. He was from Argentina and his concept of a working woman was 'barefoot and pregnant.' The big problem came when the division managers and their assistants had their yearly meeting. I was told that I could not go because I was a woman, and that his wife would not approve! I had traveled with men at IBM, and it never crossed my mind that there was a problem. Shortly after, in May 1971, Rod decided that he wanted to start his own business, and he wanted me to come with him. I agreed.

"I can't believe how much I have changed in the past ten years. I was very much a wallflower, afraid of people, and the thought of client contact was very frightening to me. I had a bad inferiority complex. I was raised in a small town, and was very shy and backward. I always felt insecure at society functions. Rod was smooth and had none of these problems, but he recognized these insecurities in me and still respected me, which was the key to our relationship. I could be myself, and he thought enough of me to support me, train me, and turn me into something else. During this time, I was beginning to understand what Rod was doing professionally. I was interested and started taking night courses at community colleges. I also did a lot of reading in his field.

"I felt a valuable part of Rod's career, and I honestly feel the company could not have survived without me. He had a terrific ego, as many architects do, and it got worse as time went on. I was the only one, including his wife, that could keep him in line, and he would take it from me. Rod respected me a lot, and I was also able to keep the employees happy. Rod had a terrible temper, and I was that stablizing force that kept things smooth. I could go to Rod and say, 'Now you have to give this person a raise,' or whatever. I did not instruct him on what to do, but I made him aware of many situations. Thus our relationship was reciprocal in many ways.

"Then he died. They found out that he had cancer in April, and on Labor Day the doctors said, 'You're not going to make it.' He lasted eight more days.

"I don't ever want to go through that again. My mother was killed in an auto wreck, but I don't think that was as traumatic. Rod and I were on the same wave length; we each knew what the other was thinking. It is a relationship that you don't ever replace in that kind of way. There will never be anybody like that to me again, no one that will know me as well during a certain stage of my life, nor be as important to me as he was. It was a very unhappy time for me.

"When Rod was dying, his wife and I were around the bed, talking about the company. Rod signed a letter asking his wife to sell the company to me, but after he died, she decided it was worth almost double what he had estimated. The attorney stated that since the letter was not notarized nor witnessed, it was not a legal document. I fought it for two months, but finally, in December, I had gotten to the point where I couldn't handle the pressure anymore. I finally told the twelve employees who worked for me, 'I want out,' and I sold my stock to another employee. I later found out they paid Rod's widow her price, but then could not make it, and went out of business.

"A lot of doors didn't open for me because I didn't have a college degree. It was often insinuated that 'you got there by sleeping with the boss—now what are you going to do?' Although this was unspoken, I felt it was what many of the men thought. I explored other fields, but nothing really intrigued me. One of the licensed architects who had worked for Rod came to see me and said, 'Why don't we start our own firm?' I remembered the trauma that Rod and I went through when we started, and I didn't want to go through that again. Then Rod's secretary came to me and said the same thing. This particular architect changed his mind shortly after our discussions, but another architect approached me, and in March 1978, we decided to jump in. We had three people and moved into an office space with two thousand square feet.

"I wouldn't go through that first year again if anybody paid me a million dollars. It was terrible! It had been relatively easy with Rod in comparison. The worst experience I had was with the bank. My husband introduced me to Security Pacific Bank where he had an account. After three months, I wanted to borrow some money, and the banker, who was about sixty, made my husband sign for my company loan! I told him we had separate property agreements and that my personal assets were far above what I wanted to borrow. The banker refused my creditworthiness completely. I was livid, but I went to my husband for his signature and had to continue to this every month. Then we needed almost double the amount, and I nearly had to have my son sign! I was finally able to find a bank (California Canadian Bank) that has given us a very large line of credit without my husband's signature or involvement in any way, which is as it should be.

"During the first year, I did not draw a salary, but the other two employees did. It was easy to get the clients; that was a 'piece of cake.' The hard thing was to get the people to do the work. It can be hard for a woman boss to get competent people to work for her. It is not the men so much as their wives. They seem to feel it is degrading for their husbands to work for a woman. But now things are going very well. We have just moved to a new location near Union Square and have 6,500 square feet, which is three times what we had. We also have grown to twenty professional people.

"An interesting side effect happened after Rod died. My husband and I almost got a divorce and actually separated for a while. Previously I had depended very much on Rod for guidance and support; we spent two hours a day talking about our various business problems. When he died, I transferred these needs to my husband. He wasn't ready for that. He had his own career and wasn't ready to involve himself to that extent in mine. We had a marriage for four years that was totally based on independence. For me to change the rules in the middle of the game was something he didn't like and was not prepared to deal with. We wound up going to a counselor, who helped the relationship get back together. But for a while, I was totally lost.

"With mentors, you can be content and happy, feel challenged, and have interesting things to do. If there is a problem, they can come to your rescue. After they die, you have to realize you are not protected and shielded anymore. Mentors can clear the air and run interference when you don't even realize it. When they die, you know for the first time that there may be people who don't like you and that are 'gunning' for you. When your mentor is powerful and likes you, then you are untouchable, as long as you please him and carry your share and support him. After he dies, there can be a real shakedown of power.

"After a mentor dies, sometimes a mentoree can do things she didn't realize she could do and probably would not have done had the mentor lived. But how do you deal with the problems after he dies?

Whom do you discuss them with? When you can be totally open, it is a relationship to be treasured; it is a very special time of life. But if you want to grow and continue, you have to leave the relationship at some time. I am finally very happy with where I am and what I am doing now.

"Looking back, it is very obvious that if I hadn't had this mentor relationship, I would still be a secretary. It never occurred to me during the relationship that I would own and be president of a successful architectural firm.

"There has never been another mentor for me. I have tried and looked, but they have always disappointed me. Something always happens to change the relationship. But I think I have come to grips with this now. I believe that my relationship with Rod was a unique thing. There was a purpose why Rod was in my life, and I also believe there was a reason why he left it. He was a strong, dominant personality, and I don't think I could ever have ended my apprenticeship. I would have always been under his thumb, and I certainly wouldn't be where I am today."

Anne Bartlow (pseudonym)
Attorney
San Jose, California

"I met my mentor, John Parkman, on an airplane. I was going to Washington in the first-class compartment, and when I returned the next night, I noticed that many of the same people were again on the airplane. I started talking to the man next to me, and we had a very good conversation with all the first-class service and amenities.

"In about two weeks I received a phone call from John, who had been sitting across the aisle. He said, "We have a need for a lawyer to work with us." It turned out that his friend had been sitting next to me, and this person had had a chance to do all the interviewing. This was in 1975, and the relationship lasted for five years. During this time, my mentor was extremely helpful. While we were close in age, John was very senior in the firm. He was very experienced in one particular way, and I was experienced in another. What John did was to help me get into the organization, and understand how the "men's club" of corporate practice works. I would go along to meetings with John to watch how he would handle board of directors' of Fortune 500 companies, and it was very, very helpful. I also noticed small things, like when he would wear his best raincoat (not his second best), and it taught me a lot.

"I helped John by giving him an honest opinion and being discreet when we discussed confidential matters. I was also much better at public relations and relating to people than he was. John was good at outthinking others, and shoving the hard ball, but often that was not enough. If he wanted something difficult accomplished, he knew that I could subtly do it, and do it well.

"The most interesting aspect of our relationship was when I decided the time had come for me to move on. About six months before my departure, I did all that I could do to alert my mentor that I was considering leaving. I took John to lunch, called him on the golf course, showed him my resignation before I sent it, and departed from the firm quite happily. But the moment I left, John stopped my mail, stopped my telephone calls, and tried to keep me from getting any of the 'perks' that came along with the partnership agreement.

"John just couldn't handle it when I left. This was obvious to the other men in the firm. They felt he was acting like a rejected suitor.

"When I was showing John my resignation, he acted like a mentor. He said, 'If I had the opportunity, I believe I would take it.' He also told me it was not in my best interest to stay, but when I actually left, he just fell apart and became extremely nasty.

"I saw John at a meeting in San Francisco several months later, and had the opportunity to see him before he saw me. I put out my hand, put a big smile on my face, and said, 'hello.' He was quite taken aback. I could see all the feelings that were rushing through him, and I felt sorry.

"My other mentor relationship ended differently, and I now have former mentors calling me for advice. One former mentor is a senior executive in a company in Los Angeles, and this man (who is sixty-five) calls me to say, 'What should I do?' It is a funny feeling. I have probably had one mentor in each job I have had—at least four or five. Each job has lent itself to a mentor; my changes have all been to higher jobs. You simply cannot *not* have a mentor. You need someone to 'help you up the steps.' Mentors have been very important to my career; I think everyone should have one.

"I think to start with, our parents are our mentors, and help us with our self-concept. I felt early in my career, from the first grade on, that I could be a winner. I have always had a lot of confidence in myself.

"All my mentors have been most helpful to me when they told me they expected more out of me than I thought I had to offer. I would think I had done the best I could, and they would say, 'You can do better than that.' I would say, 'No one else is doing it better,' and they would say, 'We are not interested in anyone else.' It was more of a stick than a carrot.

"I now am trying to find a mentor again. I have never sought one before. I have always just 'fallen into it.' I am having problems because of my level of experience. It will have to be someone who has 'seen it all' and is no longer in the fray, someone who can sit back and say, 'Here's what I would do, here is how I see you, and here is what I believe you can and cannot do.' But I have not found anyone yet. I read about organizations of prestigious retired executives, and how they helped start up companies. It seems to me that it would be fun to call them up cold and say, 'I want a mentor!' But of course I wouldn't do that! It is interesting as you get older how helpful you realize a mentor can be.

"I have been a mentor to both men and women. There are people now, some older, who both telephone me as well as discuss things in person. I worry about where they are going, and what they should do next. I have also had two mentorees who have felt they outgrew the relationship. They signaled they wanted to be friends but didn't want to be told what to do. In both these relationships, I was senior in our careers, but the age was about the same. I can see why some mentors have a problem handling the breakup of this kind of relationship. It can be hard to give up being a tutor, not to have power and control over another person, especially when it has been gratifying for a long time.

"It can be hard to find someone who has something to offer and who is willing to help you and wants to see you succeed. I have had some people offer their assistance in good faith, but instead, they really set me back. It is difficult to find a competent advisor. If you can have a model—a mentor—I am absolutely for it."

CHAPTER SEVEN

Men and Their Mentors

Lois's mentor was a woman. They spent a lot of time discussing her ideas, aspirations, and the whole feminist movement. During this time of tremendous growth, Lois later stated that she was simply dazzled by her mentor.

Several months ago, Pat was having a particularly difficult time at work and called her mentor, a female, to complain. Pat told her she was absolutely burned out. Soon, a dozen long-stemmed red roses arrived. She later wondered if a male mentor would have done this, and if not, what would he have done instead?

HOW MEN SELECT THEIR MENTORS

BOYHOOD COACHING INTO MENTORSHIP   Men are trained from earliest boyhood how the right coach can guide them. It is no wonder that they move easily into a mentor relationship. In fact, men actively seek the right mentor and seem to know how and where to go to find them. They almost never choose their bosses. They make sure their mentor has "power" and is plugged into the "action line." Organizations which do not foster the right climate for "coaching young people along" have a difficult time hanging on to their brightest talents who seek this assistance.

INSIGHTS BY DANIEL J. LEVINSON   In this chapter, I will quote periodically from Yale psychologist Daniel J. Levinson on men and their mentors, because I agreed the most with the conclusions of his research and feel that he has great insights into the male mentor relationship.

When a young man finds a mentor," according to Levinson in *The Seasons of a Man's Life*, "he is excited and spurred on by the shared sense of his promise. Yet, he is also full of self-doubt: can he ever become all that both of them want him to be? At different times—or even at the same moment—he experiences himself as the inept novice, the fraudulent imposter, the equal colleague, and the rising star who will someday soar to heights far beyond those of the mentor."[1] Thus there can often be conflict right at the start in the male/male relationship, which, according to my survey, is not true of the female/male one. Also, men feel early on that they can surpass their mentors; my respondees did not enter into their relationships with these feelings.

Levinson notes that men select mentors who are ordinarily eight to fifteen years older, a person of greater experience and seniority in the world of the mentoree.[2] While the majority of women in my study also tended to do the same, a larger group selected mentors close to their own age (no doubt because males the same age are traditionally ahead of women in experience and in position). If women select men who are twenty or more years older, there is the danger of entering into a father-daughter relationship. Also the older mentor may be removed from current problems facing the younger work force.

FEELINGS OF AFFECTION   Young men select mentors for whom they feel a great deal of affection. The words "love and adoration" are often used in describing the relationship. Here I would like to quote from an article in the *Harvard Business Review* (July-August 1978) called "Every-

---

[1]Daniel J. Levinson, *The Seasons of a Man's Life* (New York: Alfred A. Knopf, 1978), p. 100.
[2]Ibid., p. 99.

one Who Makes It Has a Mentor." This often-cited article discusses the mentor relationships of three successful males (Franklin J. Lunding, George L. Clements and Donald S. Perkins), all of whom became chief executive of the Jewel Tea Company. The study points out their belief in the importance of mentors.

When discussing the mentor relationship, Perkins was asked if he expected sponsors to get emotionally involved. He replied, "If you are asking me if you can work with people without love, the answer is no. On the other hand, if you are asking if it is possible to help people grow by expressing love only in terms of permissiveness, by never hurting them and never being candid with them, the answer is also no. So sponsorship is somewhat like parenthood."[3] Mentors do get emotionally involved; it is a person who adores you and had such confidence in you that you have confidence in yourself.

This article also bears out the fact that most CEOs feel they were "hand picked" and given special tutoring by the current CEO before they assumed the position. This brings up another topic that needs to be addressed: "being picked" versus doing the picking (also refer to the chapter on "Selecting a Mentor"). This article was one of the first of a limited number on mentors, and while these CEOs felt chosen, younger professional people, convinced that a mentor is critical, are leaving no stone unturned in their search to emulate the CEOs at the top.

Levinson sums up the relationship by saying, "The mentor relationship is one of the most complex, and developmentally important, a man can have in early adulthood." And in all the available readings, I have never once come across any exception to the rule that all high-level men have had exclusively male mentors.

HOW MEN USE THEIR MENTORS

Men use their mentors in much the way women do, with some marked differences. Men seem to divide the benefits of their mentor relationship into four general areas and expect all four to occur. Women generally accept the relationship if only some of these benefits work and have not expected or pushed for assistance in all.

---

[3]Eliza G.C. Collins and Patricia Scott, "Everyone Who Makes It Has a Mentor," *Harvard Business Review,* July-August 1978, p. 100.

BEGINNING ORIENTATION   The first area in which men feel they benefit from their mentors is during a beginning orientation in the new organization. Here, the male protegé gains from such mentor action as "he helped me to plan my career path," "he shared with me the benefit of his experience," "he gave me the push to make it happen."

SPECIFIC AID   The second benefit for younger men is more definite, and I call it specific aid. In this regard, the mentor "recommended me to my boss for promotion," "gave me visibility and approval through his trust and association," and "gave me technical knowledge necessary to improve my job."

PROTECTION   The third area is that of protection. Here I have been told that my mentor "defended me against unjust criticism," "spoke in favor of me," and "took my side in professional battles." The business world is not a fair one, and mentors can be of great assistance in this arena.

LONG-RANGE ASSISTANCE   Finally, the fourth type of help was in long-range assistance. Men said their mentors "got me on committees of high visibility with wide-reaching effects," "recommended me and helped me change positions and/or companies," and "gave other general assistance which set up my career for life."

HOW MEN LET GO OF THEIR MENTORS

According to Levinson, the male "mentoring relationship lasts perhaps two to three years on the average, eight to ten years at most."[4] As to its conclusion he says, "most often an intense (male) mentor relationship ends with strong conflict and bad feelings on both sides. The young man may have powerful feelings of bitterness, rancor, grief, abandonment, liberation and rejuvenation."[5] Men seem to understand more than women that the relationship is temporary, shorter-lived, and will come to an end. Women hold on to their mentors longer than men do, and, according to my survey, often longer than is good for their careers.

According to Levinson, the average male mentor relationship

---

[4]Levinson, *The Seasons of a Man's Life*, p. 100.
[5]Ibid.

most often ends with strong conflict and bad feelings on both sides (only 7 percent of the respondents to my survey terminated their relationship due to conflict). Other reasons included a geographical move (slightly under half of the women I surveyed ended the relationship due to the mentor's geographical move), a job change within the organization to an area other than that of the mentor's (and creating a need for another mentor), death, or natural cooling-off.

Men more than women say that they got out of the relationship because they felt "constrained." Men more often than women voice, "My mentor was beginning to take the responsibility for my own progress." And they felt this went so far as the mentor getting credit for ideas that they had not even discussed, but ideas that were lifted from their written work.

In letting their mentor go, Levinson continues, men seem to echo, "The mentor he formerly loved and admired is now experienced as destructively critical and demanding, or as seeking to make one over in his own image rather than foster one's individuality and independence.[6] The mentor, Levinson adds, voices that he finds his protegé "inexplicably touchy, unreceptive to even the best counsel, irrationally rebellious and ungrateful."[7] And so it ends. There is usually some truth in each one's feeling of resentment.

Men are also seldom willing to have a mentor relationship much past the mid-forties. In the forties, men are more interested in developing talents under them. Although there are, naturally, some exceptions, women are not as likely as men to have as many people under them, and thus my research showed women are pleased to have this relationship and are willing to continue it well past forty. Women need to be more aware that there is indeed a time to "let go". Not only must they be willing to do this but they need to know how. Harsh words don't necessarily have to follow; women can simply stop turning to their mentors for help and do their best to find a more suitable and even higher mentor better equipped to assist with current problems and future challenges.

[6]Ibid., p. 101.
[7]Ibid.

MENTORS TEACH MEN DIFFERENT SKILLS

MEN — LEARNING LEADERSHIP AND RISK-TAKING   There is strong evidence in my survey of over 400 professional women to suggest that male mentors are teaching their female mentorees different skills than their male mentorees. Research leads me to conclude that high on the list of valuable forms of assistance mentors provide to men are:

developing leadership

developing the ability to take risks

giving direction

providing information about what is going on.

WOMEN — GETTING ENCOURAGEMENT AND SUPPORT   According to my survey, women say their mentors were the most beneficial in:

giving encouragement and support

instilling confidence

providing growth opportunities and opening doors

giving visibility within the organization.

We can draw some interesting conclusions. Women seem to need and are given more support and encouragement (perhaps due to their social conditioning), whereas men are more interested in learning aggressive skills such as leadership and risk-taking, and this is precisely what their mentors are doing for them.

I think once again we need to reexamine the fact that only 6 percent of the top jobs are held by women. In reviewing the comments that top male executives made in the three articles below, the conclusion seems inescapable that male mentors are indeed mentoring differently, or why wouldn't more women be at the top?

The first two articles I refer to appeared in the *Harvard Business Review,* one in the summer of 1978 and the other in the winter of 1979. Cited earlier, the first one entitled "Everyone Who Makes It Has a Mentor," related the experiences of Jewel Tea Company key executives and their belief in the importance of mentors.[8] The second, "Much Ado About Mentors," confirmed (from a male's point of view) the experiences and beliefs of the Jewel executives, in which they agreed that having a mentor is crucial if you want to get ahead. In the third article, Gerald R. Roche, president of Heidrick and Struggles, Inc., a management consultant firm, conducted a survey of top executives mentioned in the "Who's News" column of the *Wall Street Journal* in 1977. He found that nearly two-thirds of the respondents had a menter. Of the 1,250 who responded, fewer than 1 percent were women. More than 6 out of 10 replied that their careers had been guided by a sponsor or mentor.[9] Roche further discovered that those who had a mentor earned more money at a younger age, that mentor relationships seem to have become more prevalent during the last twenty years, and that those with mentors are happier with their career progress.

CASES

The cases of Lois and Pat were selected to point out differences in the relationship that they felt were unique in having a woman for a mentor, and to reinforce the difference between male and female mentors.

Lois R. Foyt
President
Real Estate Arts, Inc.

"My mentor is Nancy Kepperman, formerly an assistant professor of political science at Stanford University, and currently president of Wellesley College. I had decided after twenty-four years away from school to go back to Stanford and finish my undergraduate degree. Nancy was one of the first people with whom I talked. I was reentering school as a nontraditional student.

"I first went to see Nancy as she was the woman contact in political science, and I wanted to talk about majoring in this area. It wasn't as

---

[8]Collins and Scott, "Everyone Who Makes It Has a Mentor," p. 89.
[9]Gerald R. Roche, "Much Ado About Mentors," *Harvard Business Review*, January-February 1979, p. 15.

much the degree as the women's movement that motivated me into returning to Stanford at this time. I felt political science would be a good field to pursue, and I asked Nancy to be my advisor.

"The mentor aspect goes above and beyond being an advisor. Nancy was one who was a sage. In our conversations, we talked about the women's movement and my consciousness, and that this was why I was back at college. I felt she had the "spirit of the age." We began to discuss things that had deep personal meaning for me. We didn't discuss what courses I would take, because that had all been outlined.

"I did not know what I would do when I got my degree. I had been working in the family business, which is an entrepreneurial-type company in the real estate business. I didn't know if I would go back into this or turn to new horizons. After I graduated, I did decide to go back into the family business, but I wanted to go back with a corporate structure. My husband was in the business, and my son, who majored in business administration at Berkeley, was joining us.

"Nancy discussed my ideas, aspirations, and the feminist movement. She knew this was one of my directions. She planned to teach a new course that would explore the idea of feminism from the political science standpoint. We talked about this course, and I learned her husband was in the political science department. I was interested in how a husband and wife worked in the same field. They had different subfields but were in the same department. I was trying to figure out what her ideas and guidelines were about this, and she helped me formulate my own ideas. This had a very far-reaching effect on me.

"I hope I was of value for her career in some way. We had good discussions and I presented a different point of view, one unlike that of most of your younger students. It was such a time of tremendous growth for me. I was able to get my political science degree and take a number of courses in related social science fields, like anthropology and sociology. I patterned the courses I took on the Stanford Center for Research on Women (CROW) outline. It was a time when I was really pursuing women's history, sex roles, and how limited views of past cultures have been. Stanford doesn't have a women's study program, but I was able to put one together. Interestingly enough, Stanford now offers a degree in feminist studies, which began in 1981-82.

"The idea of going back to school at this particular time in my life was really a growth period. I think when you have a situation with a mentor, it can be a rocky thing. It is not smooth sailing, and no one taps you on the head and says, 'I am going to pave the way for you because I have all this power.' The relationship can be emotional and, at times, also an angry one.

"After I finished school, the mentor relationship ended in some ways. If I want to see Nancy now, I cannot just drop in. It takes a formal telephone call to make an appointment. But we do keep up with letters. It is a more formal relationship. I have come a long way, but I do not yet see her as a peer—I am still dazzled by her. Nancy, as the recently installed president of Wellesley College in Massachusetts, has a great opportunity and will be brilliant.

"She was always receptive to discussing things that were happening. Since I am married and work full time with my husband, I realize at the time I had this mentor relationship, I was very involved. Growth experiences with a mentor can be brought to other personal relationships, and it has worked well with my husband and me in business. We are a good team and complement each other well. Currently we are developing specialized housing for women and single adults in the local areas. I learned so many practical things from Nancy. I have her to thank for taking time to mentor me while I formulated my ideas and values more concretely, and for helping me understand and feel a part of the whole feminist movement."

Patricia Marriott
Product Marketing Manager
Apple Computer

"I have been at Apple Computer for two years, and before that, with IBM and Hewlett-Packard. I have had few heroes, but only one mentor in my life. However, Carol Fowler falls into both categories. She is now president of Datalex, a software development company in San Francisco but at that time was a product marketing manager at Hewlett-Packard. I met her when I interviewed at HP in 1976. She dazzled me: I am tall and she is tall, I am smart and she is smart. I looked at her and thought, 'My God, a tall, smart woman *can* find happiness!'

"When I was a teenager, being tall and 'brainy' were not good things to be and did not do much for my popularity. Although I went through engineering school, a marriage, and a job at IBM, in 1976 I was still relatively naive about my own potential. What my mentor Carol did was to open my eyes to the possibilities.

"When I met Carol, I had just received my masters degree in computer science from Berkeley and had recently divorced. I went through a good deal of trauma in leaving Berkeley. I was into 'truth and beauty' then, and I wasn't sure I wanted to reenter the ugly world of business. One thing was certain—I would never go into sales or marketing. Those departments, I was sure, were inhabited by pushy, sleazy people. Yet there was Carol, sales department manager, and she destroyed that image. She is aggressive and tough in business but is a warm and genuine person.

"I joined HP in the software development lab largely because I was so impressed by Carol, and a mentor relationship soon developed. She introduced me to several women's networks and, in particular, the Math/Science Network. This group sponsors conferences for high school girls tI did not see that being a female made any difference. I had an idea, and I felt that it could be successfully exploited. I fo present career information and provide role models. The first time I saw Carol speak at one of these conferences I was dazzledhave to do is go for it, and you can get it all.' She was an incredible inspiration to me. In fact, to this day I frequently go to meetings just to hear her speak.

"Carol moved up to product marketing manager at HP, and over the years she urged me to get into marketing. I thought that was utterly ridiculous, particularly since I had no public speaking ability and very little self-confidence. I grew up in a very poor family, and the only thing my parents *did* instill in me was that I had to get a good education and work hard in school. So I got the concept early on that 'hard work pays off'—and it does!

"In 1978, I left HP to return to IBM as a systems programmer. About one year later, IBM announced that my group was to be moved to Dallas, so I went out looking for another job. I was now seriously considering Carol's advice about marketing. Software development was beginning to bore me and I was ready to try something new. One of my former managers at HP was now a vice-president at Apple Computer and he asked me to come in for an interview. When I told him I was interested in a marketing position, he had me speak to the man who was then CEO and is now President. The CEO asked, 'How would you like to work for me as manager of market research and planning?'

"At that time, I was not at all comfortable with what sounded like a high-risk situation. Apple was relatively unknown, having only 400 employees. I'd been used to the security of large corporations such as HP and IBM, and the thought of starting a new career in a small company terrified me. I spent long hours with Carol discussing my future.

"A wonderful thing about Carol is that she never tells you what to do. She asks questions—though, relevant questions. And usually there is one question that makes everything crystallize and the answer suddenly becomes obvious. It is incredible to be able to talk to someone like that. It's almost like going to a psychiatrist! She makes you see all the possibilities, and then everything seems to fall into place.

"I did decide to join Apple, and it was the best decision I've ever made! After two years and several promotions, I think I have the perfect job. If I could choose my own position right now—anywhere in the world, at any company, at any time and place—this is what I would do. In terms of my personal growth, I have learned more at Apple in two years then I could have anywhere else in ten years. We have gone public, divisionalized, introduced new products, and grown enormously! And along the way, I have discovered that I enjoy taking risks and responsibility.

"I honestly believe that without Carol's encouragement I would never have had the confidence to go with Apple, or even into marketing, for that matter. Her support at that time made a crucial difference in my career.

"It's not just height that we have in common. Our backgrounds are remarkably similar. Carol has a master's degree in math. When she was in college in Texas, women were not allowed in the engineering program! She started her career in the lab doing software development but switched to marketing when she realized that was the seat of money and power. At first I was upset by her outspoken desire for these 'corrupt' values. I felt there was a definite conflict between 'truth and beauty' and 'money and power.' But I am now absolutely convinced, as is Carol, that you can have it all! I believe the sky is the limit!

"Several months ago I was having a particularly difficult time at work. I was completely burned out, and called Carol to bitch. The next afternoon, a dozen long-stemmed red roses arrived with a note: 'Listen kid, just make youself a cup of tea, sit down, relax, contemplate how good you *really* are, and get back to basics.'

"Before Carol, I had never thought much about mentors. It soon became obvious that Carol was filling that role for me. Other people have helped in my career, but at a much less significant level. I admire her because she is a real mover and a risk-taker. She is truly inspirational! But what I think is most important is her understanding. When she says, 'I know just how you feel,' it's more than an expression of sympathy. I know she *really* understands because she has been there. It's very satisfying now to reverse roles sometimes so that Carol can call me after having a terrible day and *I* can say, 'I know just how you feel.' Sometimes this listening can be the best thing one can do for another.

"Recently at work someone commented that I 'acted just like a man' in a particular difficult situation. I was totally taken aback, yet it was meant as a compliment. It made me realize how much I have changed from the quiet, retiring person I used to be. In many ways, Carol has provided the model. She is powerful and influential, but she had not given up her human side.

"I'm glad I did 'grow up' to be like Carol. I'm in a similar job, I now make presentations at work and to outside organizations (without a twinge of stage fright), and I am providing guidance to some up-and-coming young women. Although I was not a kid when I met Carol, I thought she embodied all the qualities that I wanted to have—confidence, independence, aggressiveness, and ease in dealing with people.

"This leads me to wonder whether we become like our mentors. Perhaps in addition to following a mentor's advice, we tend to copy their styles and values. Or do we choose a mentor in the first place whose style and values are similar to our own?

"Back in 1976 when I first met Carol, I thought, 'She has got it all.' Now I know better. She makes mistakes and falls apart sometimes just like I do. One night when we had dinner she confided that she had recently gone home and cried. I thought, 'Oh my God, my hero!' Now I realize it is all right to make mistakes once in a while. You can be human and frail underneath. And I'm glad, because I think the best mentors and the best heroes are human after all."

CHAPTER EIGHT

On Becoming a Mentor

Sue stresses that she mentors women for the good of the organization as well as for their own good. Later, after she had been a mentor for a while, she realized clearly that women are not as quick to pick up on this kind of helpful relationship as men.

During her residency in psychiatry, Miriam realized how difficult it was to find women as mentors in her field. Later, as a mentor herself, she believes that there is a difference in the quality of the relationship between men and women as mentors.

When Virginia started her own high technology company, she knew of no other woman in a similar position. Later, when she became a mentor, she stated that even extremely competent entrepreneurial women sometimes need an extra push and their courage reinforced, and this is what she is able to do.

MUST YOU BECOME A MENTOR?

GOOD FOR YOU AND THE ORGANIZATION   One hopes that, after knowing all the advantages that a mentor can provide your career, professional women are completely sold on the idea of becoming a mentor at the proper time. Not only is it good for you, but it is good for the organization to develop its next generation of leaders.

Especially, if you are fortunate enough to have found a good mentor in your own career and have progressed sufficiently up the ladder, you should agree that it is only fair to have a turn at being a mentor, and be willing to share with and teach others. Good mentors consider themselves a teacher more than anything else. They teach skills necessary to solve problems; mentors encourage their mentorees to observe their own style, but to develop one which is appropriate for themselves.

Don't Wait to be Asked   Because I feel so strongly about mentorship and believe that there are many women "out there" who do understand all the rules, I feel that women leaders should not simply wait to be asked to be a mentor. Especially where they have attained higher, influential positions, they should actively seek out bright junior women and offer them support and encouragement in every possible way. With one-fourth of the M.B.A. graduates in 1981 women, they are an important crop worth cultivating! Women should try to get their mentorees on important committees, try to open doors for them, share information, and introduce them to the corporate politics in the organization. They should also try to see that their protégées have some contact with other professional people outside the office, whether at informal lunches or social occasions. As men know, much important business is conducted casually over meals!

No Longer a "Queen Bee"   Sometimes women in high positions are not as sought out as their male counterparts to be mentors. Not everyone likes women at the top, and there can be strong feelings of jealousy and resentment. Women in the same organization (even the same division) can be their worst enemies, and I have seen women being destructive to each other over and over again, and end up sabotaging their own chances of success. This seems to happen so much more often with women than with men. How many times have we all heard of the Queen Bee syndrome, "I got there by myself and, by George, I am not going to help *anyone*"? Concerned with their own survival, women have even used the excuse that they did not help or mentor other women because (due to their insecurity) they did not want their superiors to think that they gave preference to females. How sad!

HELPING YOUR MENTOREE

GIVE THOSE BELOW A HAND   Since it has only been fairly recently that women have reached high levels in any sufficient numbers, it is only of late that they have been able to reach down and give those below a hand. This spirit of helpfulness is beginning to seep down throughout the organization, especially to the mid-levels where women are the most competitive, and consequently assistance is needed most.

I believe women can be just as effective as male mentors, maybe even more so, because they understand the woman's struggle, the many outside responsibilities which most of us have, and the handicap that we are under in an organization by just being a woman. Even if a senior woman does not currently have a mentoree, at least she can be a role model or a most supportive peer.

What else can you do? Try to give your protégée the freedom to challenge not only *you*, but also the organization. In order for your mentoree to be able to do this, you will need to confide in her, share information, and let her know in general what is going on. Teach her to take risks, and let her know it is acceptable to fail on occasion, and that you will still champion her.

RECOGNIZE TALENT EARLY   Early on try to recognize women with outstanding talents and abilities and identify them for special opportunities. Let these women know that they are appreciated, being watched, and give them every opportunity to use their skills. Help them, but allow them to do things for themselves.

On one hand, you need to encourage a protégée to have patience if the organization does not move her as fast as she would like and, on the other hand, to help her get and stay on the fast track. You need to assist her in developing her personal philosophies within the organizational one.

A female mentor's counsel is especially crucial in advising women to accept a new position. Important factors should be discussed, such as: Has the new boss supervised high-level professional women before? Will they be treated with the same respect as the men? Will they be supported by their peers? Where is the power? What skills are needed to succeed? Although these questions are hard to answer, female mentors will have been in similar positions before and can help their mentorees assess the overall climate for supporting and promoting women in general, and thus be able to make a rational decision as to whether or not the promotion is best for them in the long run.

Traditionally, of course, mentors were men because they were the only ones with power. Men were certainly the only ones who could give advice on taking a high-level promotion because, until recently, women mentors had not been in high places.

WHAT MENTOREES CAN DO
FOR YOUR CAREER

LOYAL DISCIPLES NEVER HURT   Mentorees, of course, will also enhance your own career. You will have disciples who will want to work for you, invite you to speak, write about and to you, who quote you and are willing to share their own creative work. Thus, it is not totally out of generosity that one is willing to help others. It can definitely be in your own best interests and can serve to get you even higher visibility in the organization.

YOUNGER "COMERS" REFLECT WISE TUTELAGE   Also, being selected as a mentor by bright young "comers" can reflect well on your own career. Mentorship is a dual relationship. Younger people can challenge your ideas and be a source of information on what is happening at the "grassroots" level. Often their ideas of solving a problem or doing a job in a different way can relect evidence of your tutelage in the eyes of company leaders. Younger people need to question and to be questioned. They need the opportunity to formulate their views, express them, and receive frank criticism. It is less intimidating at the beginning to present their ideas to one who is supportive. The sooner that women at all levels realize this, the farther it will take them.

One of my mentors once told me: "Mentors serve that function without compensation—at least without tangible compensation. The reward is essentially psychic; namely, the satisfaction of having recognized high potential while it was still in a development state; and the still greater satisfaction of seeing one's protegée achieve through fulfillment of that potential."

CASES

Having experienced the rewards of succeeding as pioneers in their field, Sue, Miriam, and Virginia were chosen as examples of women who then became mentors themselves.

> *Susan J. Gilbert*
> Vice President
> Finance & Administration
> Syva Company (Syntex)

"I work for Syva, a rapidly growing company which is a subsidiary of Syntex. My title is vice president of finance and administration, and most of my job is fairly general. My peers and I are responsible for the strategic direction of the company, and we spend most of our time with this as well as with functional areas.

"Some of my mentor relationships have been ongoing; others have been more temporary, while the women I mentored worked for me or in my department. Some women have not been quick enough to pick up on what I was trying to do.

"I don't see much difference in the quality of the mentor relationship offered by a man versus a woman. From the mentoree's standpoint, assuming that her mentor is at a fairly high level in the company, it would not make any difference if her mentor was a man or a woman. However, a woman mentor has more experience with situations that are uniquely female, such as discrimination, if any, and raising families.

"The main thing I do for a mentoree's career is to give her the benefit of my experience. There is a distinct culture in each organization, as well as in organizations as a whole, and often younger executives coming in do not understand this. This introduction to organizational life is one area where I can be most helpful.

"While I have never terminated a mentor relationship, I believe this would not be difficult to do. As long as your protegée is successful and you are helping her, the relationship just naturally continues. When it no longer becomes useful, then I think you sense it. I have also seen some relationships end when the woman surpasses her mentor; when this occurs, I hope that she will find someone higher up who can help her. Also, at some point, many women outgrow the need to have an advisor on the side.

"When I mentor someone, I mentor to both their strengths and weaknesses. What I try to do is tell them when they are performing well and then, when they approach something incorrectly, I try to help them by suggesting a more appropriate way.

"What characteristics do I look for in selecting women to coach? I look for people who are good—very good. I look for women (and men) who have the potential to grow with the organization. Basically, you are there for the good of the organization, and if you can give junior people guidance, this will strengthen the organization. It will be in everyone's best interest. I simply look for someone, female or male, who is simply *good*, and a real asset to the company, and then I try to get them on a faster track than they might otherwise be on.

"What I find interesting is that the women I do this for are not always aware of what I am doing. Very few women pick up on the fact that you are trying to help them. Sometimes they are naive, sometimes defensive—even resentful in some cases—of the fact that you are trying to help them. They may be afraid of your approach and back off, or may even be blind to it. Certainly it is not appropriate to say, 'Young woman, I am only trying to mentor you.' Of course, I wouldn't do this! If they are clever enough to pick up on the clues you give, then the relationship can continue; they will be appreciative and will be back for more. Men are more clever in this regard than women. In fact, they will seek you out. Many women are just not tuned in to the fact that there is such a thing as a mentor.

"As to how being a mentor benefits my career, I do not personally gain a great deal. I have had a lot of experience managing people over the last twenty years, and with this kind of experience, I just would not pick up a lot by helping a more junior person, or by discussing their perspective of a particular situation. I mainly mentor because it is good for the organization and may be helpful for my mentorees' careers. It could help move them along more quickly.

"I have been assisted very much in my own career by mentors and find that they are very helpful. The man who is now my own boss has always given me a lot of encouragement. However, at the beginning, I must admit that I, too, was naive and did not know what he was doing or how beneficial this help would be. Today I have a very supportive relationship with someone who is my peer, although he is somewhat senior to me; this person has been very helpful and continues to be. I know that I can rely on his advice when I need it.

"Women who want to be helped by mentors in their careers need to be a little more open to the suggestions of others more senior. Also, I find that, if you are not comfortable taking advice and ideas from others, you probably won't be comfortable giving help when your time comes to be a mentor."

Miriam Kahn Yost, M.D.
Psychiatrist
Private practice

"I believe that there is a difference in the quality of the relationship between men and women mentors. One difference is that the relationship can be closer between two women, and another is that two women can have a more open relationship.

"It is hard to find women as role models and/or mentors in my field of psychiatry. I had a mentor figure during my residency whom I admired a great deal. The relationship meant much more than just learning from her.

"Mentors make very important contributions beyond just being role models. They show that women can achieve high positions as a result of education and hard work. Mentors can discuss all the options and possibilities that are out there. Women can admire each other as learned persons, persons of accomplishment, and even as persons of high income.

"For my mentorees' careers, I helped them clarify their goals. Most of them, of course, were younger, but a few were my contemporaries in age. One in particular was a radiologist before she was my supervisee; the key in our relationship, as in many others, was our experience, not our ages. In some ways, excellence in the medical field is even more important to women because we are looked at more closely than the men. I tried to work with my mentorees in areas outside the purely scholastic, such as teaching them to think before they speak, be thoughtful, be well read in their field, and to pay very close attention to the patient's needs. We also talked about personal goals. I am proud of the people I have supervised and mentored. What is important is that the person wants the relationship and has an open mind to learn. When this occurs, I can raise their plane of knowledge and consciousness.

"Because of the professional situation, the supervisorial assignment terminates in one year, and thus mentoring in this context is structured. On a less formal basis, I am not sure that the relationship ever ends. As a mentoree, I feel free to call my mentors, and I feel the same way about my mentorees calling me. We continue to learn and grow from each other.

"At this point, more people have sought me out to be their mentor than I have sought out as mentorees. This is mostly because of the structure of the residency program; the younger people have an opportunity to request whom they wish to supervise them. However, now I am doing something unusual and unique in my field, and I don't believe any other woman in the West Bay area is in this area— orthomolecular psychiatry. There are a few male M.D.s also doing work in the San Francisco area. I am interested in talking to people about this field and give preference to mentoring women rather than men.

"When people are really interested in their health and nutrition, I enjoy expanding their knowledge. When someone is excited about what I am doing, then I am willing to give them a lot of time. Thus, I also enjoy mentoring outside the residency program. So far, at the end of the formal part of the mentor relationships, I feel that both my needs and the mentoree's are met. I believe both parties were realistic at the beginning, and that the expectations were successfully dealt with in the process.

"As far as mentoring to one's strengths or weaknesses, the clinical assignment speaks to both about equally. Psychiatrists especially need to know their own weaknesses and what they are capable of handling. If they don't feel good about themselves, they will not be able to have as much empathy and be as helpful to others. If they have weaknesses, I suggest they go into therapy; it can be very helpful for a psychiatrist to find out what it is like to be a patient. As a mentor, it is important to know where your mentoree is in his or her development, and how fast you can feed them! I am very open in the relationship and tell my mentorees what I feel they need to change, so that there are no surprises behind their backs.

"For my career, being part of the clinical faculty assures me that I am keeping abreast of things, and mentoring young people lets me know what the next wave is thinking. Being a mentor reinforces how much more I know now than when I was a third-year psychiatric resident. What a vast difference the years of experience make!

"The learning relationship that I had at home with my parents could have been better, and to have a good learning relationship with a mentor who did not function by putting me down was a welcome change. It was very helpful. It took me a while to feel safe enough to expose myself and to discuss my mistakes, as there is a lot of trust involved in the relationship. The mentor relationship can be compared to good therapy, a good friendship, and a good family relationship—one where people boost, support, and encourage each other. For growth and development, it is absolutely essential to have mentors, and I am glad that women are beginning to be in the position to be mentors.

"In general, mentors are really very important. They can make a huge difference in one's career. As a doctor, I can reinforce my mentoree's external educational process as well as her internal growth. For myself, a mentor was the single most important factor in my wanting not only to be a fine psychiatrist, but an *excellent* psychiatrist. For me, to have someone who was very supportive, who could look at me objectively and not criticize me, was extremely important!"

Virginia S. Weinman
High Technology Entrepreneur

"The field of entrepreneurship in high technology, of which I am a part, is a pioneer field; most of the successful people in this field have been men. Females as role models and mentors simply have not existed. In fact, I know of no other successful woman in this area who is currently acting as a mentor.

"As for my background, I have always worked in data processing and over the years have developed a certain expertise. I worked with both the U.S. government as well as with IBM. I always knew that I would be an entrepreneur, and over a period of time, I became one. In 1971, I spun off and started my own software company with a small capital expenditure. Seven and a half years later, it was acquired by another computer company. During this time, we grew from a one-person shop to a six-million-dollar-a-year software company, nationally recognized in some areas.

"While I was the only woman I knew who was starting her own high technology company, I did not see that being a female made any difference. I had an idea, and I felt that it could be successfully exploited. I felt I had what it took to succeed. In fact, it never occurred to me that I would *not* be successful! I had enough confidence in myself, my ability, and my ideas to know that I would be. And indeed I was!

"I have recently enjoyed being a mentor to a younger women entering the field. Sometimes these women, who are extremely competent, seem to need an extra push to jump out and make it on their own; they seem to need their courage reinforced, and this is what I am able to do. I am able to tell them that truly there is a pot of gold at the end of the rainbow. We discuss my experiences, and ways in which they can be as successful as I have been. If they are considering such a high risk, then to begin with they need a great deal of courage. I encourage this courage!

"Also, I am able to offer some practical suggestions. For example, women entrepreneurs must be aware of the many benefits offered by the Small Business Association (SBA) and by the government through government-subsidized loans offered through the banks. They need to get to know their banker personally. I try to emphasize the risk-taking aspects; many women have not been trained to take risks as much as their male couterparts. I also point out the emotional rewards as well as the financial ones, and other rewards such as independence, freedom, and self-esteem.

"Sometimes I play the devil's advocate, and discuss the many things that could go wrong. There are many 'how-to' books, and I don't try to compete with these. What I try to do is discuss things that one doesn't find in these books. We discuss the emotional commitment, the aspects of doing the books at night after the last trash can has been carried out, the dangers of not keeping on top of the accounts receivable, and the long hours that are involved. Being an entrepreneur is certainly not a nine-to-five job! We also talk about the sacrifices of the home and social life. One cannot do everything, and big sacrifices must be made in these two areas.

"Because of my visibility and the nature of my position, I feel that the younger women select me as a mentor, rather than the other way around. I am more attracted to women who are driven to be successful, who are ambitious, talented, educable, and who have obviously high technology skills. I am definitely selective about who I help. Most of my protegées are five to ten years younger than I; none have been older.

"Most of my mentor relationships are intense and for relatively short times. The nurturing relationship is not as useful once my mentorees have started their own companies. Once they have received close counseling during their start-up and find that they are succeeding, they are almost too busy for this kind of relationship! They continue to call me, and occasionally I call them as I follow their careers with interest, but the close relationship ends.

"As far as the expectations in the relationship, I feel that they are met. My expectations, as well as theirs, were that I would encourage and advise them, and they would be successful. I feel very strongly that women can be successful as entrepreneurs.

"In starting the mentor relationship, I first play to their strengths. If they have obvious weaknesses, they will come. I need to ascertain where their skills are. The close relationship carries over to other areas as well. We discuss all kinds of conflicts that can develop, and even talk about such intimate subjects as their personal sex lives. They trust me, and it is a caring relationship.

"For my own career, the younger protegées have not had a direct benefit, but I have experienced great satisfaction in seeing them achieve success on their own. I have the emotional satisfaction of feeling a responsibility for advancing their careers.

"I wish that I had had a mentor or even a number of mentors during my career. I think it would have been most helpful. Mentors are important and could have helped me avoid a number of pitfalls. However, I don't know of any women who could have been a mentor to me. In my field, there just weren't many pioneer women. In contrast, my husband Barry, who was in the same field, had mentors. Mentors always came to him and offered assistance; it did not seem fashionable for the same mentor to sponsor a woman. Now, twenty years later, all this has changed.

"We all need a shot of encouragement once in a while, and mentors can play this role."

CHAPTER NINE

Mentor Questionnaire and Results

INTRODUCTION

A survey of the literature on professional women and their mentors suggested to me that little has been written on the subject. I decided to design a questionnaire that I would give to a large sample of professional women to study the total relationship with their mentor.

My first sample consisted of the membership of the Peninsula Professional Women's Network (NET), a prestigious group of executive and professional women in the Palo Alto area (with salaries ranging from roughly $20,000 to over $100,000); and second, the membership of the Bay Area Executive Women's Forum (BAEWF), an elite San Francisco-based network. The women were in the fields of business, law, medicine, government, or related fields.

Lastly, to expand the sample, I added individual women of achievement in major cities across the United States. Over 400 questionnaires were returned. As far as I know, this is the only sample of this size of professional women regarding their mentor relationships. All during this study, I was overwhelmed with the enthusiasm expressed by the participants and their comments that the study was long overdue.

117

Out of this research, certain very interesting and valid conclusions can be drawn.

I am going to call my sample "typical" of the professional working women population, when in fact, they are probably atypical. This group is undoubtedly superior to most random samples of working women.

QUESTIONNAIRE

BACKGROUND ON THE DATA BASE The sample was characterized by women of achievement with higher than average incomes, education, economic conditions, and status within their profession. All women did not answer all of the questions; out of the possible 400 responses, the average question got some 390 replies. Respondents were given a choice of signing their name or not. About one-third chose to identify themselves, and even added an extra comment that I should call them if I needed further information. I should also add that some question- naires were returned by women who had *no* mentors. These were not counted. And finally, my goal was to receive 400 questionnaires, and those over this number were not counted either.

The first question in the survey regarded the respondent's age. Some 398 participants responded and 49 were under thirty, 243 were from thirty-one to forty, 72 were from forty-one to fifty, and 34 were from fifty-one to sixty. None were over sixty-one.

When asked about their education I received 397 responses, and the participants were asked to indicate their highest degree. Some 28 women replied that they have from two to four years of college (but no degree), and 118 hold undergraduate degrees, 175 have Masters, 55 have Ph.Ds, 10 have J.D.s, 9 are M.D.s, and 2 hold D.D.S.s. Thus 63 percent of the sample have advanced degrees.

The category on salary was interesting. Some 395 women replied, and 157 women fall into the range of $21,000 to $30,000; 150 women made from $31,000 to $40,000; 37 from $41,000 to $50,000; and 51 made over $51,000 (with some considerably higher than $100,000). This is probably in line with professional salaries in general for the female population, but undoubtedly considered less than professional males make.

When surveyed on their economic background, these women have risen a great deal as adults from their status as children, reflected in the answers of some 394 replies. When indicating their economic background as children, 45 women checked "poor urban, or rural," 170 checked "lower middle class," 167 checked "upper middle class," and 12 checked "wealthy." However, as a professional adult, their economic backgrounds improved greatly. None checked "poor urban, or rural," only 15 checked "lower middle class," the largest number, 360, checked "upper middle class," and 19 checked "wealthy." This would appear to indicate that they had been responsible, at least in part, for their own economic rise.

Religion was the next question and was answered by 392 respondents. Some 170 women replied that they were Protestant, 60 replied that they were Catholic, 42 Jewish, and 120 listed no preference. Probably a survey of this kind would not have had so many women reply "no preference" some ten years ago.

The marital status turned out to be a surprise, and with 390 replies, only about half of the women are married (exactly 200), and the other half divorced (105) or single (85).

I thought one of the more revealing questions on the survey came out with regard to the participants' number of children. Of the 394 who answered, over half of the women in the study had no children! Some 220 marked no children, 80 marked one child, 47 marked two children, 27 marked three children, and 20 marked four or more. No responsibility in the child-rearing area undoubtedly leaves both more flexible time for work as well as longer available hours.

As far as job classification of the 387 respondents, 247 began as professional, and 140 started as nonprofessionals and "worked their way up."

CURRENT VIEWS ON MENTORS   When asked about the contributions of mentors to their careers, 389 responded; 225 women checked "very valuable," 112 marked "some value," 30 marked "limited value," and 22 put "no value." This was in contrast to the next question of a mentor's value to careers in general, and here (of a total of 391 replies), 312 women marked "very valuable," 62 marked "some value," 17 put "limited value," and no one put "no value." Thus professional women clearly see the value of a mentor relationship, but many have not been able to find a mentor who has made this outstanding contribution to their own career.

When asked if their mentors had been men or women, of the 393 responding, some 296 women replied, "men," 17 women put "women," and 80 checked "men and women." I feel this answer is certainly typical of professional women everywhere. The women were then asked to comment on whether or not they felt mentors were more valuable to men than to women. With 392 responding, 230 replied "about the same," 27 stated that mentors were more important to men, and 135 said that they were more important to women.

As to the question whether, in addition to mentors, women have had role models, 413 replied yes; 83 replied affirmatively to having had helpful peers and other teacher experiences. Thus women seem open to learning and eager for this kind of help.

The next question unified almost everyone. When asked if they thought men's mentors were mostly men, 387 put "yes", none put women only, and only 2 put "men and women equally."

The group was split over the question, "have your mentors been your boss?" Of the 360 replying, 185 put "yes" and 175 put "no." But to show professional women *do* know the rules, of the 381 answering the next question "should mentors be your boss," 299 replied "no" and 82 said "yes." It would appear that women are sophisticated in this area, but just have not been able to find the ideal mentor.

There were three questions under "what started the relationship," and of the 388 women replying, 75 stated that they "selected" their mentors; 236 replied that they "fell into it" and 77 responded that they "had been selected." Thus it appears that not enough thought is going into who selects whom, and that the respondents have not been assertive enough in their search for a mentor.

When asked "how many mentors have you had," of the 389 responding, 108 women replied "one," 133 women responded "two," 80 said "three," and 68 said "four or more." As far as their mentor's age, 389 replied, and 10 women said "younger," 50 said "same or slightly older," 141 said "5 to 10 years older," 116 said "11 to 15 years older," 37 said "16 to 20 years older," and 35 stated "over 20 years older."

As far as the duration of the relationship, 383 women answered, and 42 responded that it lasted "one year," 162 said "two to three years,"

47 replied "four to five years," and 132 stated "over five years and still continuing."

It was interesting to find out why the relationship with their mentors ended. Some 388 women tackled this question, and 80 said it was "still going on," 25 stated the "mentor died," 177 said that he "moved geographically," 79 said that he "moved within the same company," and 27 said there was "conflict." When asked if they had a mentor outside the workplace, 390 answered with 174 women checking "yes" and 216 responding "no."

The question of sex is a lively topic, and of the 381 replying, 99 women admitted having sex with their mentors while 282 said "no." But when asked if they advised it, of the 357 who answered, *all* responded "no." And interestingly enough, 357 was the smallest sample who responded to any of the questions! Could this be an area of conflict to those not responding? Or perhaps some women were offended, or chose not to answer such a personal question.

The participants form a cosmopolitan group, as proved by the response to the question "how many times have you changed jobs?" Of the 389 responses, only 20 replied that they had never changed jobs, 57 said "one or two," 200 said "three or four," and 112 said "five or over."

When asked how many bosses have you had, 394 replied; 10 women said "one," 82 women said "two or three," 80 said "four or five," and 222 said "over five."

One question which surprised me greatly in the survey was "have you ever surpassed your mentor?" Of the 373 women who answered, 197 said "yes," and 176 said "no." This answer was unexpected, considering that men have higher level jobs than women; perhaps the women felt that they had gained all that they could from the relationship, and even if they did not get a higher promotion, they had surpassed their mentor in all the ways in which he could continue to teach them.

The last question in this section clearly showed the progress of women in the late decade. The answer of these 387 women plainly put them out of the "Queen Bee" syndrome of the 1970s and squarely into the 1980s. When asked "would you be willing to be a mentor," 315 said, "feel strongly and would go out of my way," 67 said "yes, if asked," and only 5 women said "undecided." Absolutely no woman said "no"! It was interesting to note that many of the women in the study added comments to the effect that they became more aware of the total mentor syndrome through sharing my research, and that perhaps they would not have answered this section so strongly before.

The qualitative data was very provocative, and I only wish there was enough room in the book to record all of it. Due to space, I chose the following responses most listed from the sample.

When asked to list three words describing the way the respondent felt about her mentor, the following comments were made (beginning with the most frequent):

a. respect
b. admiration
c. trust/confidence
d. loyalty
e. support
f. friendship
g. appreciation
h. awe
i. resentment

When the respondents were asked to "list three ways in which their mentors have helped their careers," they wrote (in order of frequency) the following sage replies:

a. taught corporate rules
b. provided opportunity
c. increased self-confidence
d. gave advice and counsel, guidance
e. got me promoted
f. put me on visible "fast track"
g. gave encouragement
h. critiqued my work
i. directed my career path
j. helped formulate career goals
k. gave recognition
l. took risks for me
m. acted as sounding board
n. spoke well of me

o. challenged me
p. gave extra training.

ADDITIONAL COMMENTS The last section in the questionnarie was optional; however, it was answered by almost everyone. Here the women were asked to make *any* comment regarding their mentors, whether or not the topic was covered in the survey. I subjectively selected the following remarks as most poignantly indicative of the sample at large. The respondees wrote:

"Mentors are more important to women; it is harder for us to get ahead."

"Women do not get mentored the way men do."

"I would have been one and possibly two levels higher if I'd had a better mentor."

"Most of my mentors have been men; I have received very little help, if any, from women."

"Particularly in medicine, a mentor can be of great benefit. There are a few of us."

"There is a marvelous 'fall out' of experience, training, and knowledge gained by being close."

"I have expended much more energy in being a mentor than when I was mentored."

"After having strong parents and strong teachers, I sought out a strong mentor. It took several years to establish this relationship, and it has been well worth the effort."

"Women who have reached my level of success do not have energy enough left over to devote to helping others along."

"My mentors gave me the most important ingredient needed for success—self-confidence."

"He realized my compulsion to work and helped channel it constructively."

"I've made several wrong assumptions about what I hoped would be mentor relationships and ended up feeling used."

"Women in government especially need a mentor; the percentage of those that survive is small."

"There was a time when I thought hard work alone would do it. Now I know better."

"When my mentor lost confidence in me, I felt it. It was a turning point in my career. Then I got mad and set out to show him."

"Mentors often don't want to be surpassed."

"Having someone to talk to makes the rough spots easier."

"My mentor told me he'd had a helpful mentor, was glad to be my mentor, and now I must return the favor to someone under me."

"The stronger I became, the weaker he seemed to be."

"Having been a mentor to several women, I made a conscious effort to get them to examine their goals and take steps to achieve this. It was one of the most satisfying aspects of my work."

"Women must learn the benefits of the mentoring relationship or drown!"

"It was impossible for me to receive help at the beginning due to my stubborness to 'do it by myself.'"

"My mentors mainly added great psychological support and helped my lack of self-esteem."

"If you are trying to make it in a big corporation, then you *must* have a mentor."

"I came to this country when I was seventeen, and immediately felt inferior. Thus later in my professional life as a dentist, a mentor was of special significance for me."

"Termination is the hardest part about having a mentor."

"Mentors are very hard to obtain."

"A mentor should also share the joys and disappointments that he experiences."

"Most men I know who are successful have had a mentor; unfortunately, women often do not have the same relationship, even though they have the same identical mentor."

"Mentors have been the key to my success."

"My mentor went so far as to buck the firm's president to promote my career."

"Not one of my peers said that he could honestly be a mentor to a female."

"My mentor provided emotional support when I went through a crisis totally unrelated to the job."

"At first, I was unaware of the potential to my career of working with a mentor; now I approach their offer of assistance more openly, and with gratitude."

"Particularly for a woman lawyer with only academic training, mentors are especially helpful in showing how to practice."

"Women should be taught, as men, that it is a positive sign to outgrow your mentor, signaling it is time to move on."

"In times when you don't have a mentor, you really need a good "Old Girl's Network."

"I respected my mentor's training and brains. When he said, 'Yes, your idea is new and significant,' it was the push I needed to follow a new career path."

"I finally realized I'd outgrown my mentor, both professionally and personally."

"I have actively looked for women mentors but haven't had much success, the primary reason being the lack of women at high professional levels."

"There should be mutual feelings of commitment in a mentor relationship."

"In turn, I feel that I have supported and even furthered the career of my mentor."

"My mentor, a woman, believed in me, inspired me, and demonstrated that I too could have a significant career."

"Never have sex with your mentor; I did and got fired."

"As a mentor, I realize how much my career has been helped by those that I have mentored."

"When my mentor died, I was wiped out. It took a long time for me to work through the pain, appreciate the benefits, and be thankful for the relationship."

"I felt so guilty when I left my mentor; he in turn acted like a rejected suitor."

"Men use mentors in an entirely different way; they are much more savvy."

"She cut the learning curve in half."

"A mentor was critical to my success."

UNFULFILLED ASPIRATIONS

While the women in the survey were pleased with the tangible results that they felt came as a result of their mentor relationships, they still voiced some even higher aspirations. In the future they would like to see their mentors (listed in order of most frequent response):

1. give them advice in getting more challenging and interesting assignments
2. help them get promoted to positions previously held by men
3. assist them in negotiating higher financial rewards
4. suggest to them ways for more visibility in own organization
5. recommend them for national corporate boards
6. recommend them for national governmental committees.

RESULTS OF THE SURVEY

Traditionally, of course, almost all women's mentors have been men, and this study reinforced this knowledge with over three-fourths of the respondents replying that their mentors were indeed men; the remaining sample had men and women equally as mentors. Only 17 had women with no men as mentors. The mentor relationship is described as almost like one of fondness and respect. It is intense, and there is mutual trust, caring, confidentiality, and a willingness to share victories and defeats.

From this survey of over 400 responses, and from my reading of the literature of men and their mentors on similar professional levels, the following broad conclusions can be drawn:

1. Women do not understand the "mentoring concept" as well as do men. They are still more "threatened" by openly sharing information and are not as comfortable in being "coached or guided." Some of this may go back to a young boy's childhood and his positive relationships with his athletic coach and teacher.

2. Studies have proven over and over again that successful men at the top echelon of their organizations believe: "mentors often determine who gets ahead," "having a mentor is crucial if you want to make it," and "everyone who succeeds has had a mentor." Men, knowing this, are trained to look for a mentor, a god-father. Women are not as sophisticated in aggressively seeking this relationship and over half who had found mentors reported that they "fell into it." Only 20 percent reported that they "selected their mentors."

3. More men than women state that they "surpassed their mentors." This is not a surprise when you note that such a significant percent of jobs at top levels are held by men. Thus women, not having the upward mobility, do not have as many opportunities to pass their mentors.

4. Men are more savvy than women in knowing that a mentor relationship is more or less temporary and transitional. Men tend to actively seek a mentor, to gain all that they can from him, and then let go of the relationship sooner than women do. (Women sometimes seem so pleased to have a "sponsor" that they keep the relationship going far after it has peaked in its effectiveness.) The male's mentor relationship tends to last around three years. Although slightly less than half of the women (42 percent) agreed, it was a surprise that over 34 percent stated their relationship lasted over five years, and some are still continuing after this.

5. By far the major cause of the termination of the male mentor relationship is conflict, with a geographical move second. Women's termination is due to geographical moves first and organizational moves second. Conflict is rarely mentioned.

6. Men almost never select their boss as their mentor, believing that the relationship should not be influenced by either their work

performance or by their opportunity to be promoted or to leave the company. Women select their boss about half of the time, according to my studies, even though they know a boss is not an ideal mentor (which can be hard to find).

7. Men have three to five mentors in the course of their working careers. Women in this sample tend to have one to three. The majority have only one at a time.

8. Men's mentors tend to be eight to ten years older than their protegés; most women's mentors were also. A significant number, 36 percent of my study, said their mentors were five to ten years older, and 29 percent said eleven to fifteen years older.

9. Feelings most commonly expressed by men for their mentors according to the literature:

   (a) admiration   (b) respect   (c) gratitude.

   Feelings expressed by this sample:
   (a) respect   (b) admiration   (c) trust/confidence.

10. Men's studies point out that mentors were valuable to them in ways they felt were unique to males. For example, the crucial role of their mentor was in:

    (a) developing leadership
    (b) developing the ability to take risks
    (c) giving direction
    (d) letting them know what is going on

    Women, on the other hand, said their mentors were beneficial in:

    (a) giving encouragement and support
    (b) instilling confidence
    (c) providing growth opportunities
    (d) giving visibility within the organization

    Thus we can draw the interesting conclusion that early on, women seem to need more support and encouragement, and men are more interested in learning aggressive skills such as leadership and risk-taking.

11. Men seldom have a mentor relationship past age 40. At this time, they turn their attention to "bringing up the bench talent under them," and in being a mentor. Women normally do not supervise as many people as men do and so far have not had as many opportunities to act as mentors. Thus they cling longer than they should to their mentor, which can be more comfortable than useful.

12. Sex and the mentor relationship was an interesting topic. While one-fifth of my respondees admitted having sex with their mentors, this was the question which most unified everyone to answer "NO" when asked if they advised it! There were many explanatory comments for their negative responses which they included with their questionnaire.

13. The answers to the last question of the survey were gratifying. When asked if they were willing to be a mentor, some 81 percent responded that they would "go out of their way," and 17 percent said that "they would if asked," and no one responded "no." This is characteristic of the new spirit of the women's movement. This will be a dominant trend in the 1980s...women not only working together, but women aggressively helping each other in their climb to the top.

CHAPTER TEN

Conclusions for Professional Women and their Mentoring Relationship

COMMON THREADS

In the preceding chapters, I examined all of the complex components that go into the mentoring relationship: the benefits to the mentoree, the gain to the mentor, the good to the organization. I tried to assess the importance of this relationship. I have also reviewed it in comparison to other professional relationships that the people involved may have.

Mentorship in its entirety may never be fully understood. What *is* known is that the results are greater than the sum of its parts. And also, that there are common threads which run throughout the relationships.

To better understand present-day mentor relationships, the survey replies of the 400 women of achievement are significant. The results could well be used to strengthen the current working bond between the mentoree and the mentor, as well as to assist in breaking the relationship when appropriate, without as great a degree of conflict.

The knowledge acquired not only from this survey, but from the case studies and the comments of the senior women interviewed, could also be useful in setting mentor/mentoree goals for the next decade.

Their experiences and insights could influence the structure and success of future relationships as well.

IMPLICATIONS FOR THE FUTURE

LONG-RANGE NEEDS   What are the implications of this research for the future? From the information compiled, the following is needed:

a. more emphasis should be put on the literature describing the importance of the mentor relationship;

b. a more penetrating kind of mentor relationship by fast track people should be recognized;

c. senior management should put more accent on professional activities that will give junior people greater contact with those on a high level throughout the organization; and,

d. an organization has an obligation to better identify the potential mentors; they need to be given more opportunities to develop talent. A mentor role enhances the power and prestige of the mentor. He should be seen more clearly in his role of inspired teacher, and wise counselor, and be given the credit due his contributions.

GOVERNMENT
Supervisor Rebecca Morgan
Santa Clara County Board of Supervisors

Rebecca Morgan, Santa Clara County Supervisor, 5th District in San Jose, and a Stanford M.B.A. states that "many women are not aware of their own personal stakes in the affairs of government and politics." She points out that few women run for public office and assume leadership roles. A political mentor could encourage his protégée to increase her participation and explore the opportunities for involvement. Rebecca states, "Politics is certainly a passage to power." She says that women are the majority of the population in the United States, and yet there is one out of 100 in the U.S. Senate, 19 out of 435 in the House of Representatives, none of 50 state governors, and 880 out of 7,000 state legislators. Women hold only 5 percent of the federal judgeships. She concludes: "In other words, while the number of women elected to public office in the last decade has quadrupled, they still hold only about 12 percent of the key positions in the United States."

Supervisor Morgan first got a taste of politics when she helped Paul N. McClosky in one of his successful races for the U.S. Congress. During this time, she got a real feeling for all that was involved in managing a campaign. She first ran in 1973 for the Palo Alto Board of Education. She won and feels that she was greatly helped by other women in attaining her victory. Many of the same women later helped with her election to the county position in 1980.

"The Board of Superisors has recently appointed a woman as the top administrator in Santa Clara County. As far as I know, she is the first female to be appointed to that position in any county of over 30,000 people. She was not appointed because she was a woman, but because she was the most qualified. I am glad I am now in a position to be instrumental in appointing well-qualified female candidates.

"When I was growing up, my most significant role model was Margaret Chase Smith, the senator from Maine. She was the only female of political prominence in the late 1950s, and I identified with her. I admired her for her integrity, common sense, and independence.

"Today I try to accept as many speaking engagements as I can and share with other women my campaign knowledge and what it is like to win. I am available to mentor other women, and often get calls for political advice. In the future, I am not convinced that more women will run; it seems like younger women today are looking for money, and they will not find it in politics. However, they will find power."

CORPORATE BOARDS
Dr. Rita Ricardo-Campbell
Senior Fellow
Hoover Institution
Stanford University

Dr. Rita Ricardo-Campbell, Senior Fellow at the prestigious Hoover Institute, is a member of several boards, including the corporate boards of the Gillette Company (whose Finance Committee she chairs) and Watkins Johnson Company, as well as the President's Economic Policy Advisory Board, the American Council on Science and Health's board of scientific advisors, and the National Council on the Humanities. She says that one way for women to achieve positions of power in the business world is to be on more corporate professional and national boards.

For example, of the top 1,300 companies listed in *Fortune,* she cites that less than 2 percent of their directors are women. Of the 16,000 people who serve on these boards, 365 are females; however, as most serve on more than one board, the actual number of women is about 200.

How can more women get on boards? Dr. Ricardo-Campbell states that there are three reasons why women are not currently serving as outside directors on more boards. Some boards do not have members who know women who have the requisite experience and competence in business or the professions. This is coupled with a general lack of visibility of those few women who have "made it." The most important reason is that there is, at best, a very small pool of women who are Chief Executive Officers (CEOs) of companies. And as previously stated, only 2 percent of the *Fortune's* top 1,300 companies have a woman CEO.

"An enlightened board chairman can make a difference in women being selected," Dr. Ricardo-Campbell says. "An enlightened board chairman is one who is convinced that women are intellectually equal to men, and who will push for women as board members.

"Enlightened chairmen must also be in positions to meet capable women and take time from their business to serve on boards and committees where intelligent and knowledgeable women are found," she states. Among the types of boards where women are numerous are those of museums, art and music associations, and university boards. Women who serve on these nonpaying, nonprofit boards may meet on equal ground those CEOs who are co-members.

Finally, Dr. Ricardo-Campbell advises women who want to get to the top to prepare by reading business journals and other related materials, and work to open up the professional clubs that are not traditionally open to women (such as was the famous Duquesne Club). Many senior women have stated that it limits one's professional contacts and opportunities not to be allowed membership in such groups. Dr. Ricardo-Campbell believes that, with more women in middle management positions today, more women will aspire to and will rise to the CEO levels.

Thus, a most beneficial way that mentors can assist professional women, and I feel this will be more common in the 1980s, is to recommend them for memberships to boards of directors. It is a well documented fact that most board members are men. In proportion to its intrinsic importance, women do not aspire to memberships as they should.

Men who are active directors extend and cross-fertilize their professional knowledge and form loyalties that reach far beyond the board room. Through these contacts, far-reaching consequences result: still more invitations to serve on other boards, recommendations to be the CEO at an even more prestigious company, and greater visibility that often results in government appointments. On this level, this kind of "who do you know" is significant.

Why are women not selected for board memberships? Take a look at the criteria. As Dr. Ricardo-Campbell states, "Most board members are CEOs of their own companies, and women are simply not at this level." The women's applicant pool is small. Women are sometimes selected as "tokens" who have risen to prominence through such fields as community service, public relations, education, or who have received recognition through their well-known volunteer (nonpaid employment) backgrounds. These women are not usually anticipated to add much substance to the board's decisions, but some women in this category have contributed greatly to the company.

The following is a much-talked-about unusual advertisement for a corporate director that once appeared in *The Wall Street Journal.* I have included it as it is typical of the criteria needed to become a board member: "experience in service on boards of directors is essential, as is experience in guiding a company in the $10 million size range to the next higher order of magnitude." The ad drew a total of fifty-five replies, but not one was from a woman.

ACADEMIA
Dr. Gail Fullerton
President
San Jose State University

Dr. Gail Fullerton, president of San Jose State University, says, "The

CORPORATE DIRECTOR

Company in greater Boston area, listed on American Stock Exchange, plans to increase the number of outside directors on its Board. Experience in service on boards of directors is essential, as is experience in guiding a company in the $10 million size range to the next higher order of magnitude.

Compensation competitive with market scale of directors' fees.

Reply in strict confidence to:

Box R-965, The Wall Street Journal

Source: J.M. Juran and J. Keith Louden, *The Corporate Director* (New York: American Management Association, Inc., 1966), p. 205.

notion of a mentor is a new enough one, although the process is a very old one. As for myself, mentors have not furthered my own career in a teaching sense, like showing me 'how to.' I have, however, been signled out at some crucial points in my career, was given a tremendous responsibility, and was told to 'go do.' Thus, I was put in a visible position and given the opportunity to show what I could do."

What are the important criteria that will help women succeed today? Dr. Fullerton believes that high on the list is energy. "Women especially need a high level of energy because anyone in a top job is going to be pulled many different ways," she says. As an example, Dr. Fullerton serves on several boards, including the Symphony, Chamber of Commerce, Scouts, and others. While women may have supportive husbands at home, as Dr. Fullerton does, nonetheless, she believes men do not expect to play the "gracious host." So women need not only the vigor to cover all bases on the job, but in the community and the home as well.

Wise use of time is another significant factor. With so few women in high-level positions, they are hampered by a shortage of time. Not as many senior women act as mentors because of a dire lack of available time. As an example, Dr. Fullerton previously mentored several women when her schedule was more flexible in earlier positions. She believes it is difficult for junior women to have much access to senior women, but she does not have a quick remedy for improvement.

Networks are important, Dr. Fullerton believes, and because of her age group, she was the only women in her class at graduate school. As a result, she always felt a part of the "old Boys' Network." She points out that there were "simply not that many women around, and perhaps for that reason, when I could later chose a woman to work with, it was an absolute delight. At one point my husband said, 'Aren't there any *women* in your network?!' And now there are.

"Of the women that I have mentored, we stay in touch after the formal relationship has ended. It then becomes almost like a sister relationship. This is as it should be. While I hate to lose good people from the University, I know I have to write references to help them move on when it is in their best interest. Once they leave with my recommendation and blessing, they become part of my new network. They continue to share their contacts and friends, and thus I expand my own knowledge and perspective."

Dr. Fullerton's last point is to advise junior women to be careful of appearances: "I think you have to be careful of appearances in the male/female relationships. In my own case, I would have been reluctant to have so obviously attached myself to a male mentor for fear it would have been misunderstood. So while I was pleased to have been chosen, pleased to undertake the tasks and assignments, I was very hesitant to have turned the relationship, as a man might have done, into a mentoring one, for fear that either he or the world might have misunderstood. Always, as you advance in your career, you have to be careful of appearances.

"In my own case, there were not any women around that I could have undertaken to ask to be my mentor. I think that may change as more women move in positions to act as mentors. I hope so."

SUMMARY ON MENTORSHIP

MENTORING—AN IMPORTANT CONCEPT FOR THE 1980s   The mentoring function is an important concept which will receive new attention in the current decade. The mentoring relationship can go far beyond the work situation and the transmittal of new skills; it can reach into areas totally unconnected with the work place and can literally elevate and change one's life.

MENTORS ESSENTIAL FOR WOMEN'S SUCCESS   Women are just beginning to realize the crucial role that mentors can have in their professional lives and are better utilizing them in their climb upward. As only 6 percent of the top jobs are held by women, they are finding out just how necessary mentors are in coaching them to compete professionally as they strive toward a share of the top 94 percent of the jobs held by men.

WOMEN NEED TO EMULATE MEN IN EFFECTIVE USE OF MENTORS   This imitation by women should be in all phases of the relationship, including the desire to have a mentor, the selection, working effectively with, and knowing when their apprenticeship has ended. Traditionally, this guidance and sponsorship has been reserved for men only.

THE MENTOR RELATIONSHIP A CYCLICAL ONE   While women need to fully understand the benefits of this relationship, they also need to know that it can be a cyclical one. There are negative effects as well as positive ones, and a woman should not continue to cling to her mentor longer than is useful to her career.

MEN NEED TO OFFER SAME RELATIONSHIP   Men who are currently mentoring women often need to realize that they are not teaching them the same skills they are tutoring men. Since men are beginning to recognize women have tremendous potential in the work force, they need to be aware that they are not coaching women in the same leadership and risk-taking skills that are critical if women are to get ahead. To date, men have not acknowledged this. Men also need to recommend competent women for professional boards and other positions of power.

SENIOR WOMEN TODAY AGGRESSIVELY SEEKING TO BE MENTORS   Senior women are to be applauded in their recent aggressive efforts to go out of their way to identify younger women to mentor. Women leaders in the 1980s will leave the "Queen Bee" syndrome behind, and not only agree when asked to be a mentor, but will seek out bright junior mentorees. Thus women are beginning not only to work together, but to actively help each other's climb to the top. This is a phenomenon that will continue to grow during the decade ahead.

ORGANIZATIONS SHOULD SET CLIMATE   Organizations, realizing the value of mentoring to the careers of both the mentor and the mentoree, should set the climate to encourage more senior women to act as mentors to bright junior women as well as to men. Juniors, well tutored, will focus their skills on the aims and needs of the organization.

Field Study Methodology

These surveys represent a search for all the components which go into the total mentor relationship. I was interested far beyond just a report of empirical research. I wanted to understand what the needs were of both the mentor and the mentoree, how the relationship began, the chemistry involved, how the relationship met the expectations of each, and how it is terminated. Or is it?

Through this book, I also wanted to further the cause of women in the professions, and to give them new tools to advance their careers. I hoped to provide a rationale for a new kind of mentorship provided by male mentors—ways that they can be even more helpful to women. And, I wanted to show, without any doubt, that mentors are absolutely crucial to the woman who wants to get ahead.

Professions in general need to make more responsible efforts to give women room to be women (we are different from men) and the opportunity to succeed at top levels. We should not continue to be held back because we are women.

139

FIELD STUDY QUESTIONNAIRE:
"VALUE OF MENTORS"

The following source of information was one of three questionnaires utilized in my research both in developing the concept and in drawing the conclusions. I designed this questionnaire after much thought to include all facets of the mentor relationship that I believed to be important. It was mailed to over 200 members of the Peninsula Professional Women's Network. It was then mailed to some 100 members of the San Francisco Bay Area Executive Women's Forum. The two groups' responses formed a definite pattern, and I was interested to see if women in other states would reply in a similar manner. Thus the third mailing was to over 300 professional women across the United States in major cities; interestingly enough, their replies corresponded with the above model.

The return was tremendous. Over 400 out of the 600 questionnaires came back. Questionnaires were counted only if the respondent had a mentor. From the replies, some interesting and valid conclusions can be drawn. Below is the questionnaire that the respondees received.

BACKGROUND OF THE DATA BASE
Category

1. Age
   Under 30   31-40   41-50   51-60   Over 61

2. Education
   2 years college   Undergraduate degree   Masters degree
   Ph.D.   J.D.   Other

3. Salary
   Under $20,000 $21,000-$30,000 $31,000-$40,000
   $41,000-$50,000   Over $51,000

4. Economic background as child
   Poor urban, or rural   Lower middle class   Upper middle
   class   Wealthy

5. Economic background as adult
   Poor urban, rural   Lower middle class   Upper middle
   class   Wealthy

6. Religion
   Protestant   Catholic   Jewish   No preference

7. Marital status
   Single   Divorced   Married

8. Children
   0   1   2   3   4 or more

9. Job classification
   Began as professional   Worked way up

TOTAL MENTOR EXPERIENCE

1. Value to your career
   Very valuable   Some value   Limited value
   No value

2. Value to careers in general
   Very valuable   Some value   Limited value
   No value

3. My mentors have been
   Men   Women   Men & women equally

4. In addition to mentors, have you had
   Role models   Helpful peers   Teacher relationships

5. Are mentors more important to men than women?
   Yes   About same   No

6. Are men's mentors mostly
   Men   Women   Men & women equally

7. Have your mentors been your boss?
   Yes   No

8. Should they be?
   Yes   No

9. If you had a mentor
   Did you carefully select him/her?   Did you "fall into" it?
   Were you selected?

10. How many mentors have you had?
    1   2   3   4 or more   0

11. Was your mentor's age
    Younger   Same or slightly older   5 to 10 years older

11 to 15 years older   16 to 20 years older   Over 20 years older

12. How long did the relationship last?
    1 year   2 to 3 years   4 to 5 years   Over 5 years or still continuing

13. Why did the relationship end?
    Still going on   Mentor died   Moved geographically
    Moved within same company   Conflict

14. Have you had a mentor outside work?
    Yes   No

15. If you had a mentor
    Have you had sex with your mentor?
    Yes   No
    Do you advise this?
    Yes   No

16. How many times have you changed jobs?
    None   1 or 2   3 or 4   5 or over

17. How many bosses have you had?
    1   2 or 3   4 or 5   Over 5

18. List three words (in order) describing your feelings about your mentor:
    1.
    2.
    3.

19. Have your ever surpassed your mentor?
    Yes   No

20. List three ways your mentor assisted your career:
    1.
    2.
    3.

21. Would you be willing to be a mentor?
    Feel strongly & would go out of way   Yes, if asked
    Undecided   No

SUGGESTIONS & COMMENTS (OPTIONAL)

Please comment on any topic of your interest regarding mentors whether or not your topic was included in the questionnaire.

_____

Name (optional)

CASE STUDY QUESTIONNAIRE: "BASIC ISSUES OF MENTOR RELATIONSHIPS"

The women I interviewed in depth were selected from the Field Study Questionnaire as those who illustrated a certain segment of the mentor relationship. They also had to be willing to discuss their relationships and agree to appear by name in the book. While I audio-recorded everything that was said in the interview, I later omitted parts that were not relevant to the sections for which the women were selected. I found these informal discussions perhaps the most valuable part of my research, because the participants were so frank and open. They were also interested in my work, felt the book would be useful, and encouraged me to finish as soon as possible—this provided my final stimulus! All the women were very outspoken on the need for professional women to have a mentor, and I consider this part of the study critical to the success of the research.

The case study women received questions in advance of the interview, and we remained close to this basic outline. The interview lasted from over one to three hours. After the material was in typed form, each participant reviewed her material for both content and accuracy. Below are the questions that the interviewees received.

1. How did you meet your mentor? What started the relationship?
2. What did he/she do for your career?
3. How did you feel about your mentor during this relationship?

4. Comment on your relationship with your mentor after the formal relationship ended (not much has been written about this, and I am anxious to pioneer some thoughts along these lines).

5. Any other comments on the relationship unique to *you*?

SENIOR WOMEN QUESTIONNAIRE: "WOMEN AS MENTORS"

In the third and final part of my research, I designed a questionnaire for very senior women who are functioning as mentors, and who are known for their outstanding achievements in their profession as well as in other fields. These women were sent the following questions in advance, and the discussion centered mostly around their role as a mentor. We also talked about their function as role models. All the women selected are mentors to men as well as to women and are convinced that the relationship is not only beneficial to their mentorees, but to the organization and to themselves as well.

They received the following questionnaire:

Assuming that you have mentored several women, I would like to ask your thoughts on the following questions:

1. In your experience, what is the crucial difference in men vs. women as mentors?

2. What do you feel were your most important contributions to the career of your mentoree?

3. How do you "select" the women that you want to mentor?

4. How do you terminate the relationship?

5. What was the "fit" between *your* expectation of the relationship and that of your mentoree?

6. How long did the relationship last?
   What was the age difference?
   Have you ever mentored a women older than yourself?

7. Do you mentor to their strengths or weaknesses?

8. What have your mentorees done for *your* career?

Tables and Graphs Depicting Women's Status

The tables and graphs that follow were chosen as being illustrative of professional women's place in the labor force, and they basically reflect the low status that females have in higher positions, regardless of the field. They were taken from two publications of the U.S. Department of Labor, *Perspectives on Working Women: A Datebook*, published in October 1980 (Bulletin 2080), and *Women in Management*, also published in 1980. The information, the most recent of this kind available, clearly shows that women will need special tutoring and mentoring if they are to succeed in these higher positions traditionally held by males.

TABLE 1   Women Nonfarm Managers and Officials
1969 and 1979 Annual Averages
(Women 16 years of age and over)

Year	Number (in thousands)	Women as percent of Total managers and officials	Total labor force	Women managers as percent of all employed women
1979	2,586	24.6	42.2	6.4
1969	1,261	15.8	37.8	4.3

Source: U.S. Department of Labor, Bureau of Labor Statistics, Employment and Earnings, January 1980, Tables 3, 21, and 22; Employment and Training Report of the President, 1980, Tables A-3 and A-16.

In private industry, the number of managers has increased from 1.3 million to 2.6 million in the past ten years. However, in 1979, women held only one-fourth of all managerial jobs, and women managers (who worked year around, full time) had a median salary of only 55 percent of that earned by men. Of persons earning $25,000 and over, less than 4 percent were women. In top-level administrative positions, women hold only 6.4 percent of these jobs.

TABLE 2   Women in Federal Government

Grade	Women as percent of total	
	Nov. 1978	Nov. 1977
GS 1 to 4	77.7	77.1
GS 5 to 8	62.2	61.4
GS 9 to 11	29.7	27.6
GS 12 and 13	10.0	9.3
GS 14 and 15	5.2	4.8
GS 16 to 18	3.9	3.4

About 626,000 women were employed as full-time workers for the federal government in 1978. These women represented 44 percent of all government workers, but their distribution by grade shows that they still hold the largest share of lower grade jobs and smaller proportions of the upper level positions. In grades GS 9 through GS 16, of a total of 22,905 managers, 93.8 percent were men, compared to 6.2 percent who were women. In the super-grade levels GS 16 through GS 18, women number only 260 compared with 6,338 men. At the local levels of officials and administrators in the state and local governments, only 14 percent were women.

TABLE 3   Women in Government

Women are the majority of the population in the U.S. and yet...	Number possible	Women	Women from Bay Area
Supreme Court	9	1	0
U.S. Senate	100	1	0
House of Representatives	435	19	0
State Governors	50	0	0
State Legislatures	7000	880	0
Federal Judgeships	100%	5%	0
California State Senate	40	2	0
California State Assembly	80	9	0

In other words, only about 12 percent of the key political positions in the United States are held by women.

Source: *Status of Women in U.S. Politics,* Office of Continuing Education, San Jose State University, 1981.

Women in the higher federal jobs fared even worse: 1 woman out of 100 in the U.S. Senate; 19 out of 435 are in the House of Representatives; none out of 50 state governors; only 880 out of 7,000 state legislators; and women hold only 5 percent of the federal judgeships.

TABLE 4   Degrees Conferred in Business and Management by Institutions of Higher Education in the United States, 1973-74 through 1977-78, by sex of student

Degrees	1977-78	1975-76	1974-75	1973-74
Bachelor's				
Total	163,274	143,436	135,455	133,905
Women	44,604	28,211	22,223	17,481
Women as percent of total	27.3	19.7	16.4	13.1
Master's				
Total	48,661	42,620	36,450	32,820
Women	8,216	4,958	3,080	2,161
Women as percent of total	16.9	11.6	8.4	6.6
Doctor's				
Total	867	956	1,011	983
Women	72	52	41	50
Women as percent of total	8.3	5.4	4.1	5.1

Source: National Center for Education Statistics

During the school year 1977-78, more than 8,000 women received their master's degrees in business and management, representing 16.9 percent of all such degrees. This is a substantial increase from prior years. Another 45,000 women (or 27.3 percent) earned bachelor's degrees in business and management during 1977-78, and 72 women (8.3 percent) received their doctorate.

As far as working for an institution of higher education, women held nearly 639,000 of the 1.4 million jobs; they were 92 percent secretarial/clerical but only 23 percent executive or administrative.

TABLE 5   Median Usual Weekly Earnings of Full-time Wage and Salary Workers by Sex, May 1967-78 and Second Quarter, 1979-80

| Year | Usual weekly earnings | | | | Women's earnings as percent of men's |
| | In current dollars | | In 1967 dollars | | |
	Women	Men	Women	Men	
May of:					
1967	$ 78	$125	$78	$125	62
1969	86	142	79	130	61
1970	94	151	81	131	62
1971	100	162	83	134	62
1972	106	168	85	135	63
1973	116	188	88	143	62
1974	124	204	85	140	61
1975	137	221	86	138	62
1976	145	234	86	138	62
1977	156	253	86	139	62
1978	166	272	85	140	61
1979[1]					
2nd quarter	183	295	85	137	62
1980:					
2nd quarter	200	317	81	129	63

[1]Data for 2nd quarter 1979 and later are not strictly comparable with previous years.

TABLE 6   Median Usual Weekly Earnings of Full-time Wage and Salary Workers by Sex and Occupation, Annual Averages, 1979

| Occupation | Usual weekly earnings | | Women's earnings as percent of men's |
	Women	Men	
Professional-technical	$263	$372	71
Managerial-administrative, except farm	235	399	59
Sales	159	311	51
Clerical	183	287	64
Craft	188	310	61
Operatives, except transport	159	253	63
Transport equipment operatives	186	277	67
Nonfarm laborers	159	213	75
Service	139	208	67
Farm	130	163	80

148

TABLE 7 Employment of Women in Selected Occupations, 1950, 1960, 1970, and 1979 (Numbers in thousands)

Occupation	Number				Women as percent of all workers in occupation			
	1950	1960	1970	1979	1950	1960	1970	1979
Professional-technical	1,946	2,746	4,576	6,519	40.1	38.0	40.0	43.3
Accountants	56	77	180	344	14.9	16.4	25.3	32.9
Engineers	6	8	20	40	1.2	0.9	1.6	2.9
Lawyers-judges	7	7	13	62	4.1	3.3	4.7	12.4
Physicians-osteopaths	12	16	25	46	6.5	6.8	8.9	10.7
Registered nurses	394	567	814	1,184	97.8	97.6	97.4	96.8
Teachers, except college and university	837	1,196	1,937	2,207	74.5	71.6	70.4	70.8
Teachers, college and university	28	36	139	172	22.8	21.3	28.3	31.6
Technicians, excluding medical-dental	21	44	49	199	20.6	12.8	14.5	16.1
Writers-artists-entertainers	50	82	229	470	40.3	34.2	30.1	37.8
Managerial-administrative, except farm	672	780	1,061	2,586	13.8	14.4	16.6	24.6
Bank officials-financial managers	13	28	55	196	11.7	12.2	17.6	31.6
Buyers-purchasing agents	6	61	75	136	9.4	17.7	20.8	30.2
Food service workers	93	141	109	224	27.1	24.0	33.7	35.4
Sales managers-department heads; retail trade	35	68	51	135	24.6	28.2	24.1	39.8
Sales	1,314	1,646	2,143	2,779	34.5	36.6	39.4	45.1
Sales representatives (including wholesale)	37	70	76	162	5.2	7.3	7.2	12.4
Sales clerks, retail	1,175	1,384	1,465	1,671	48.9	53.7	64.8	70.7
Clerical	4,273	6,263	10,150	14,152	62.3	67.5	73.6	80.3
Bank tellers	28	88	216	458	45.2	69.3	86.1	92.9
Bookkeepers	556	764	1,274	1,740	77.7	83.4	82.1	91.1
Cashiers	187	367	692	1,298	81.7	78.4	84.0	87.9
Office machine operators	116	225	414	677	81.1	73.8	73.5	74.9
Secretaries-typists	1,494	1,917	3,686	4,681	94.6	96.7	96.6	98.6
Shipping-receiving clerks	19	24	59	103	14.3	8.6	14.3	21.3
Craft	236	252	518	737	3.1	2.9	4.9	5.7
Carpenters	4	3	11	16	0.4	0.4	1.3	1.3
Mechanics, including automotive	21	25	49	49	1.2	1.1	2.0	1.4
Printing	35	35	58	101	11.8	11.0	14.8	22.2
Bakers	14	17	32	61	12.2	15.9	29.4	43.6
Decorators and window dressers	14	24	42	94	32.6	46.2	58.3	72.9
Tailors	16	8	22	12	19.8	20.0	31.4	34.3
Upholsterers	5	6	10	12	8.3	10.0	16.4	21.4

TABLE 8   Labor Force Participation Rates of Women and Men,
Annual Averages, 1950-79, and January-June 1980

| Year | Participation rate (Percent of population in labor force) | |
	Women	Men
1950	33.9	86.4
1951	34.6	86.5
1952	34.7	86.3
1953	34.4	86.0
1954	34.6	85.5
1955	35.7	85.3
1956	36.9	85.5
1957	36.9	84.8
1958	37.1	84.2
1959	37.1	83.7
1960	37.7	83.3
1961	38.1	82.9
1962	37.9	82.0
1963	38.3	81.4
1964	38.7	81.0
1965	39.3	80.7
1966	40.3	80.4
1967	41.1	80.4
1968	41.6	80.1
1969	42.7	79.8
1970	43.3	79.7
1971	43.3	79.1
1972	43.9	79.0
1973	44.7	78.8
1974	45.6	78.7
1975	46.3	77.9
1976	47.3	77.5
1977	48.4	77.7
1978	50.0	77.9
1979	51.0	77.9
January June 1900	51.2	77.2

TABLE 9 Occupational Distribution of Employed Women,
Annual Averages, Selected Years, 1950-79

Occupation	1950	1960	1970	1979	Women as percent of all workers in occupation, 1979
Total: Number (in thousands)	**17,340**	**21,874**	**29,667**	**40,446**	**41.7**
Percent	**100.0**	**100.0**	**100.0**	**100.0**	**—**
Professional-technical	12.5	12.4	14.5	16.1	43.3
Managerial-administrative, except farm	4.4	5.0	4.5	6.4	24.6
Sales	8.7	7.7	7.0	6.9	45.1
Clerical	27.8	30.3	34.5	35.0	80.3
Craft	1.5	1.0	1.1	1.8	5.7
Operatives, including transport	19.6	15.2	14.5	11.5	32.0
Nonfarm laborers	0.8	0.4	0.5	1.3	11.3
Service, except private household	12.4	14.8	16.5	17.2	59.1
Private household	8.7	8.9	5.1	2.6	97.6
Farm	3.6	4.4	1.8	1.2	18.0

TABLE 10   Managers and Administrators,
by Selected Detailed Occupation, 1979 Annual Averages

Occupation	Total employed	Women employed	Women as percent of total
	(in thousands)		
Total	**10,516**	**2,587**	**24.6**
Office managers, n.e.c.	416	263	63.2
Restaurant, cafeteria and bar managers	632	224	35.4
Bank officials and financial managers	620	196	31.6
Buyers and purchasing agents	451	137	30.4
Buyers, wholesale and retail	200	80	40.0
Sales managers and department heads, retail trade	339	135	39.8
School administrators, elementary and secondary	299	112	37.5
Officials and administrators, public administration, n.e.c.	414	110	26.6
Health administrators	185	89	48.1
Managers and superintendents, building	152	76	50.0
School administrators, college	116	38	32.8
Officials of lodges, societies, and unions	113	33	29.2
Sales managers, except retail trade	347	30	8.6
Credit and collection managers	55	22	40.0
Inspectors, except construction and public administration	104	13	12.5
All other managers and administrators	6,273	1,110	17.7

Note: N.e.c.—Not elsewhere classified. Source: U.S. Department of Labor, Bureau of Labor Statistics: Employment and Earnings, January 1980.

TABLE 11 Women Employed as Managers and Officials in Private Industry, by Selected Industries, 1978

Industry	All managers	Women	Women as percent of all managers and officials	Women as percent of all workers in industry
Total, all industries	**3,539,506**	**601,514**	**17.0**	**39.6**
Agriculture, forestry, fisheries				
Agricultural products, crops	4,054	265	6.5	33.9
Agricultural products, livestock	1,348	86	6.4	37.3
Agricultural services	3,797	320	8.4	25.6
Forestry	1,530	50	3.3	16.7
Fishing, hunting, trapping	228	7	3.1	18.3
Mining				
Metal mining	9,503	162	1.7	7.3
Anthracite mining	792	10	1.3	3.7
Bituminous, coal, lignite mining	18,651	197	1.1	4.2
Oil and gas extraction	30,814	1,088	3.5	14.7
Nonmetallic minerals, except fuel	7,922	193	2.4	8.1
Contract construction				
General building contractors	13,374	713	5.3	10.7
Heavy construction contractors	23,388	695	3.0	7.9
Special trade contractors	9,778	544	5.6	6.8
Manufacturing				
Food and kindred	122,659	8,413	6.9	29.7
Tobacco manufactures	6,749	581	8.6	33.5
Textile mill products	54,957	5,073	9.2	47.4
Apparel and other textile products	36,416	12,072	33.2	78.9
Lumber and wood products	30,461	1,425	4.7	17.0
Furniture and fixtures	22,640	1,795	7.9	32.6
Paper and allied products	56,763	2,985	5.3	22.6
Printing and publishing	66,760	11,041	16.5	38.5
Chemicals and allied products	150,605	9,385	6.2	25.3
Petroleum and coal products	30,910	1,055	3.4	16.9
Rubber and miscellaneous plastics	47,768	2,888	6.0	33.2
Leather and leather products	15,983	3,140	19.6	60.5
Stone, clay, glass products	47,445	2,253	4.7	22.7
Primary metal industries	107,288	2,906	2.7	10.2
Fabricated metal products	96,819	5,002	5.2	22.1
Machinery, except electrical	181,618	9,383	5.2	20.3
Transportation equipment	194,310	6,902	3.6	16.0
Instruments and related products	56,449	5,812	10.3	41.9
Miscellaneous manufacturing industries	22,771	3,361	14.8	50.8

(con't)

TABLE 11 (continued)

Industry	All managers	Women	Women as percent of all managers and officials	Women as percent of all workers in industry
Transportation				
Railroad transportation	26,540	473	1.8	6.1
Local and interurban passenger transit	5,311	488	9.2	20.1
Trucking and warehousing	57,383	3,213	5.6	12.8
U.S. Postal Service	838	237	28.3	42.7
Water transportation	8,828	454	5.1	12.0
Transportation by air	31,196	3,520	11.3	31.5
Pipelines, except natural gas	1,995	38	1.9	11.1
Transportation services	5,837	1,074	18.4	39.9
Communication	136,826	42,795	31.3	47.5
Electric, gas, and sanitary services	88,791	4,066	4.6	16.7
Wholesale trade				
Durables	100,990	7,768	7.7	26.0
Nondurables	70,181	7,257	10.3	39.1
Retail trade				
Building materials and garden supplies	10,072	1,162	11.5	31.7
General merchandise stores	245,958	108,458	44.1	68.2
Food stores	112,833	16,988	15.1	40.4
Auto dealers and services stations	15,207	1,176	7.7	19.4
Apparel and accessory stores	29,416	12,371	42.1	69.5
Furniture and home furnishing stores	12,381	1,639	13.2	37.7
Eating and drinking stores	75,111	18,607	24.8	56.6
Miscellaneous retail stores	37,147	8,735	23.5	57.8
Finance, insurance, real estate				
Banking	219,070	68,160	31.1	66.9
Credit agencies, except banks	41,462	10,564	25.5	62.0
Security, commodity brokers, and services	11,587	1,418	12.2	38.2
Insurance carriers	128,008	27,895	21.8	29.8
Insurance agents, brokers and services	7,181	1,196	16.7	57.3
Real estate	9,366	1,945	20.8	41.0
Combined real estate, insurance, etc.	414	87	21.0	38.3
Holding and other investment companies	5,179	566	10.9	41.3

(con't)

Services

Hotels and other lodging places	26,497	7,754	29.3	50.9
Personal services	12,170	3,997	32.8	59.5
Business services	109,493	14,632	13.4	34.5
Auto repair services, garages	7,430	933	12.6	29.8
Miscellaneous repair services	1,839	106	5.8	18.3
Motion pictures	4,338	734	16.9	41.2
Amusement and recreation services	8,066	1,499	18.6	38.8
Health services	160,289	93,824	58.5	80.1
Legal services	2,363	872	36.9	59.9
Educational services	3,280	1,011	30.8	54.0
Social services	11,462	5,088	44.4	64.0
Botanical gardens, zoos, museums	1,363	421	30.9	45.7
Membership organizations	12,473	3,262	26.2	56.2
Miscellaneous services	46,006	2,848	6.2	23.9

Source: Equal Employment Opportunity Commission, unpublished data.

GRAPH 1   Labor Force Participation Rates of
Women and Men, Annual Averages, 1950-80

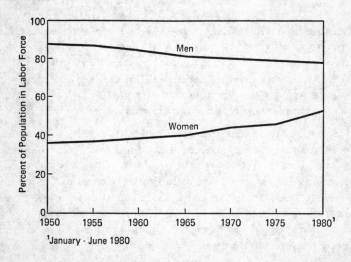

[1]January - June 1980

Projections in industrial and technological expansion indicate continued growth in managerial occupations throughout the 1980s, and women are a major resource for helping to meet the demand for these workers. A total of 7.1 million job openings are expected to occur for managers and administrators, which is a 21-percent expansion in these areas. Growth is particularly projected in some of the industries where women are already employed in large numbers, and where they have had some success in moving to higher levels (health administration, banking, building, building management and superintendency, school administration, and office management).

However, the United States has entered the 1980s facing severe economic problems including inflation, recession, and uncertainty concerning the supply and price of energy. The economic climate which supported the strong labor force growth of professional women in the 1970s is changing, and there are already indications that the growth of all women participants may be slowing. It is unclear what this will mean to professional women. The labor market bears close watching, for it is hoped that women's experience will differ considerably from the past and that opportunities will grow as projected.

LABOR FORCE, EMPLOYMENT, AND UNEMPLOYMENT

The extraordinary increase in women's labor force activity that characterized the 1970s continued unabated through practically all of 1979. Nearly 12 million more women were in the labor force in 1979 than in 1970; these women accounted for about 60 percent of the gain in the labor force. Areas of considerable change in the 1970s which are bound to affect women's labor force participation in the 1980s include:

AGE   Women 25 to 34 years old accounted for nearly half the increase in the number of female workers during the 1970s. A remarkable 64 percent of all women 25 to 34 were working or looking for work in 1979, and the first half of 1980, including 54 percent of the mothers in this age group who had to juggle the responsibilities of home and child care with those of a job. The pattern of a more continuous work history for women in these ages may widen their career and advancement opportunities in the 1980s.

CHANGING JOB MIX   Although the majority (55 percent) of employed women began the 1980s in traditional clerical and service occupations, a substantial number had made inroads into professional-technical jobs with higher status and earnings, e.g., doctors, lawyers and accountants. In 1970, 60 percent of all female professional-technical workers were in the more traditional areas of nursing and precollege teaching; by 1979, this proportion had dropped to about 52 percent.

UNEMPLOYMENT   About 2.9 million women were unemployed in 1979, an increase of around a million since 1970. The unemployment rate for women, which had climbed from 5.9 percent in 1970 to a record high 9.3 percent at mid-decade, had dropped to 6.8 percent in 1979. As in past decades, unemployment rates generally remained higher for women than men, with the gap widening when business was buoyant and declining during sluggish periods, such as the first half of 1980.

WOMEN NOT IN THE LABOR FORCE   Women constitute about 7 of 10 persons outside the work force. For the most part, these women state that they do not want a job, reporting household responsibilities as the main reason they neither work nor look for work. However, as greater proportions of younger women enter the labor market, the women who do not work for pay outside their homes are increasingly older; in 1979, the median age age of women not in the labor force was about 51 years, compared with a little more than 45 years at the beginning of the 1970s.

GRAPH 2   Unemployment Rates of Women and Men, Annual Averages, 1950-80

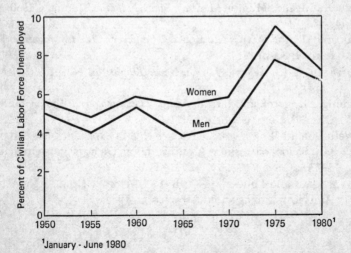

[1]January - June 1980

Bibliography

Collins, Eliza G. C., and Scott, Patricia. "Everyone Who Makes It Has a Mentor," *Harvard Business Review*, July-August 1978, pp. 89-101.

"The Corporate Woman," *Business Week*, February 25, 1980, pp. 85-91.

Epstein, Cynthia Fuchs. *Woman's Place*. Berkeley, CA: University of California Press, 1970.

Foxworth, Jo. *Boss Lady*. New York: Warner Books, 1978.

Fury, Kathleen: "Mentor Mania," *Savvy Magazine*, January 1980, pp. 42-47.

Halcomb, Ruth, "Across the Board," *Conference Board Magazine*, February 1980, pp. 13-18.

Harragan, Betty L. *Games Mother Never Taught You*. New York: Warner Books, 1977.

Hennig, Margaret, and Jardin, Anne. *The Managerial Woman*, Garden City, NY: Simon & Schuster, 1977.

Jewell, Donald O. *Women and Management: An Expanding Role*. Atlanta, GA: School of Business Administration, Georgia State University, 1977.

Juran, J. M., and Louden, J. Keith. *The Corporate Director*. New York: American Management Association, 1966.

Kanter, Rosabeth Moss. *Men and Women of the Corporation.* New York: Basic Books, 1977.

Larwood, Laurie, and Wood, Marion. *Women in Management.* Lexington, MA: Lexington Books, 1977.

Levinson, Daniel J. *The Seasons of a Man's Life.* New York: Alfred A. Knopf, 1978.

McLane, Helen J. *Selecting, Developing, and Retaining Women Executives.* New York: Van Nostrand Reinhold Company, 1980.

Missarian, Agnes K. *The Corporate Connection: Why Executive Women Need Mentors to Help Them Reach the Top.* Englewood Cliffs, NJ: Prentice-Hall, 1982.

Profile of a Woman Officer. Heidrick and Struggles, Inc. San Francisco: 1980.

Roche, Gerald. "Much Ado About Mentors," *Harvard Business Review,* January-February 1979.

Scheele, Adele M. *Skills for Success.* New York: William Morrow and Company, 1979.

Sheehy, Gail. "The Mentor Connection: The Secret Link in the Successful Woman's Life," *New York Magazine,* April 5, 1976.

Stead, Bette Ann. *Women in Management.* Englewood Cliffs, NJ: Prentice-Hall, 1978.

Strober, Myra H. *Bringing Women into Management.* New York: McGraw-Hill, 1975.

Trahey, Jane. *On Women and Power.* Avon Books, New York, 1978.

"Women Finally Get Mentors of Their Own," *Business Week,* October 23, 1978, pp. 74-80.

Women's Bureau, U.S. Dept. of Labor, *Women in Management.* Washington, D.C.: Government Printing Office, 1980.

Woodworth, Margaret, and Woodworth, Warner. "The Female Takeover: Threat or Opportunity?" *Personal Administration,* January 1979, pp. 19-28.

Index